FINDING PERFECTION IN LIFE'S
IMPERFECTIONS

Finding Perfection in Life's Imperfections

It's All a Matter of Perspective

SHAWN J. SHILLINGFORD

CONTENTS

I would like to dedicate this book to my grandmother, Kathleen "Kay" Weber

~ 1 ~

FOREWARD

December 21, 2019

Thank you for taking the time to pick up this book. My name is Shawn Shillingford. In my thirty plus years of life, I have experienced quite a lot. It is currently four days before Christmas, and I am listening to some of the most beautiful, beloved songs ever produced for the season. I imagine many people are frantically rushing around, trying to find the "perfect" present. Many others are racing from one home to another in an effort to "check off" an item on their "to do" list. I myself am doing a bit of procrastinating. I *should* probably be studying lines for my scenes in an upcoming film I am working on tomorrow. Perhaps I should at least attempt to wrap some of the gifts that I bought for my friend John and his mom Marie.

The truth of the matter is that I know these things are going to get done, so why stress myself out how and when they get done? Does it honestly matter? No, I really do not think it does. 2019 was quite a year, to put it bluntly, and right now I think the world could use a bit of enlightenment so to speak.

Before you say to yourself:

"Who is this guy and why should I care what he thinks?"

I ask you to consider this point: What is your worldview? Are you really living your life or are you merely existing? There is definitely a difference between the two. Living is getting out and truly being in the moment. Existing is sitting back, passively waiting for things to happen to you.

I look around and see "experts" and "celebrities." Who are these people and why do we give them such credence? Famous people and those in positions of power have only achieved what they have due to other people.

I am not cynical of others' power or influence. I am simply making the case that their voices are no more valid than yours or mine. Therefore, let me get to the purpose for this book: to hopefully help *you*. It truly is my belief that one of our main purposes here on this planet is to help one another.

You may mind my writing style a bit laid back and casual. For me, it is important to be relatable and conversational. I want you to feel as if you and I could be having a discussion together somewhere while you read.

Now, let me provide you with full disclosure: I am **NOT** a licensed medical professional nor do I pretend to be. The thoughts and ideas in this book are mine, with a few exceptions. Other authors' words will be quoted.

Before we get started, let me provide you with a bit of information about myself, your guide through this book. I am a son to Charles and Lisa, grandson, friend, cousin and nephew. I have been employed in restaurants, retail stores, cafeterias, schools, and summer camps.

I have been to Europe, addressed Austrian Parliament, visited Canada on Canada Day, and worked with young student athletes at a camp for the visually impaired in Tucson, Arizona. While in Hollywood, California as a seventeen-year old, I was approached by an actress in the 1939 classic film *The Wizard of Oz* who wanted me to study at her Academy of Dramatic Arts.

I have been in various films, including one in which I appeared as a Nazi, which was filmed in the dead of winter in Saratoga Springs, NY, later to be viewed by actual Concentration Camp survivors. I have also been to an actual concentration camp.

I've met *Mickey Mouse* at Disney World and have been inducted into numerous academic societies. I published a book *You Never Know...*, which I have been fortunate enough to present to some of my personal entertainment heroes. I have accomplished some of my dreams and other milestones I have yet to accomplish.

I am an only child. I have never been married. I have never had children. I have never been a property owner. I have never yet lived on my own.

We live in a world where some own so much, yet others own nothing, where appearances are "everything" and character and principles are admonished. In the following pages, many using personal anecdotes and analogies, I will share with you my personal beliefs, as well as joys and heartaches and the lessons I have learned along the way. I wish it were possible to cram all of my thoughts about life together, but I fear I would never finish. Life is, after all, finite if nothing.

Therefore, sit back, relax, and in some of the imperfections presented in this book, learn to find the perfections in life's imperfections.

~ 2 ~

COMPARISONS

"Don't compare your beginnings to someone else's middle." -Tim Hiller

The more I see in this world, the more I am convinced that comparison is one of the roots of evil and unhappiness. It plants its seeds in our subconscious and suddenly we become aware of something we *do not* have, which ultimately leads to one of the Seven Deadly Sins: envy. Think back to when you were little and innocent. How often were you aware of status? I would be willing to bet very little if you go back far enough in your memory bank. I am going to give you a very basic example.

I remember when I was probably around ten or eleven. I was completely oblivious of the brand of shoes or clothing that I wore. As a matter of fact, I *hated* going shopping with my mother when it came time to buy clothes.

However, one day at school, some of the other kids started making fun of my clothes. I was not wearing (insert whatever "name brand" you wish here), and somehow, I was made to feel inadequate. At that point, I suddenly became aware of being different. I was being shamed through someone else's lens of "acceptable" and suddenly, I began to question my clothes because of someone else's insipid opinions of "fashion."

That may sound like an overly simplified example of comparison, and it may be. However, consider this: how often are *you* inundated by someone else's idea of "perfection?" I am going to guess daily. The "perfect body," "perfect family," "perfect life," "perfect job," or "perfect children." Sometimes, it may be a bit more subtle and people do not even realize how a simple statement could lead to a negative comparison.

For instance:

"George just got accepted into (insert name of college or university). Out of twelve thousand applicants, only one hundred and fifty were accepted."

Well, what happens if George's friend overhears this conversation and he was one of the eleven thousand eight hundred fifty others who *did not* get accepted, even though it was one of his *biggest* childhood dreams (We will discuss dreams gone awry in a later section. Many ideas in this book will overlap because, like life itself, it is not always neat, tidy, and organized). Suddenly, due to comparison, George's friend feels inadequate and depressed although there were probably a "million and one" other factors outside of his control that determine why he was not accepted.

Think about some of the comparisons that you make in your own mind. What purpose do they serve to you? Would you say they make you happy or unhappy? If they are holding you back (and chances are good they probably are limiting you), discard them with the rest of the garbage in your life. The only person you should ever compare yourself to is the person that you were yesterday. That is all *any* of us can do.

~ 3 ~

CHANGE

"The only constant in life is change." -Heraclitus

Whether or not you like change, it simply is a fact of life. Change is something that is guaranteed. It is something that can leave you feeling excited and inspired by the possibilities of something new, or it can paralyze you with fear of the unknown. It is also impossible to control. Human beings like to try and control as much as possible: aging (change), profession (change), other people (change), and even the weather (change). If you took note, in that list I put the word "change" in parentheses next to each one of my examples. Change is the underlying theme of each one and the irony of the fact is that we often attempt to prevent or cause change by manipulating the changes ourselves. It is kind of crazy to think about, is it not?

I guess the point I am trying to make to you is that change is a force of nature. The very essence of being a living, breathing being means that every single one of us is going to encounter quite a bit of change on our personal journeys. Although some change will be classified as "good" and some will be classified as "bad," knowing that each and every one of us experiences change means that it is a shared experience which bonds all of us together. That is a beautiful thing.

One final thought on this topic and it is a definite contradiction and perhaps even a bit of a cliché:

"The more things change, the more they remain the same." The older one gets, the more apparent it becomes that change is cyclical and many times eventually evolves back to an original state from the past.

~ 4 ~

MATERIALISM

"Materialism is the only form of distraction from true bliss." -Douglas Horton

As I sit and write, I am reflecting on the fact that tomorrow is Christmas Day. Children all over the world are dreaming tonight of the presents that Santa Claus will be delivering. It is true joy to experience the magic of Christmas through a child's eyes. Christmas, from a materialistic point of view really is a child's holiday.

Christmas, of course, is really about the birth of Jesus Christ. The actual day of Jesus' birth is not believed to have been in December. Over the years, and through various cultures and traditions too lengthy to describe in detail for our purposes, the blending of Jesus' birth and Saint Nicholas' (later to be popularly known as "Santa Claus") spirit of giving to others formed the tradition of giving while simultaneously celebrating the Lord's birthday. How does this tie into materialism?

Christmas no longer in its' true spirit always comes to represent peace, love, and family. It has grown into a largely secular holiday driven by greed and materialism.

Earlier today, in keeping with both the spirit of the season and a new sense of enlightenment which I am *very* eager to share with you, I could not help but think of some of the wonderful memories I had associated with some material goods over the years. While looking at my toy cars, I was immediately transported to earlier, simpler times in my life, some of which correspond to loved ones no longer physically present.

Materialism, however, can distract us in our lives. It also can lead to one of the Seven Deadly Sins: gluttony. There is a saying which alludes to the fact that we come into life with nothing and leave with nothing except the life we lived. It is an absolutely true statement.

Consider, for example, the "Greatest Generation" of United States' citizens that lost many, if not all, material goods and financial security during the Great Depression during the early part of the twentieth century.

Also consider the millions of victims of the Holocaust during World Word II that not only lost entire families (an unimaginable atrocity), but additionally all financial and material resources. Then take into consideration starving children all over the world without access to food and water. Let us also not forget about people who lose everything in some other kind of tragedy (fire, hurricane, etc.) All of these events are very real and people unfortunately experience them all of the time.

In my personal opinion, the only types of material goods that truly matter are essential survival items and ones that are irreplaceable such as pictures, homemade family heirlooms, etc. The rest is simply a distraction, none of which we can take with us when we die.

My final thought on this topic was quite possibly informed when my grandfather passed away and it took over two years to clean out and sort through his home. The late comedian George Carlin perfectly summarized this all too common human fallacy in a piece entitled *A Place for My Stuff.*

As for me? I could live in a one room shack with the bare essentials I previously stated and I know I would be just fine. Material goods do not define me, and they do not have to define you either.

~ 5 ~

HAVING IT ALL

"The secret of having it all is loving it all." -Joyce Brothers

It is Christmas night and I am sitting at home right now, quietly relaxing. The beautiful twinkling lights and sense of peace and joy are abundant in the air. The most important gift, cherished time with loved ones, is in the forefront of my mind. It is almost as if time has come to a standstill, which I am sure is something each and every person has fantasized about. It is about as close to a "perfect" a feeling as exists for a human. If only this could be life at all times. If only...

I was reminded of a story from earlier this year today during a talk with my father. On a day when I am reminded to "count my blessings," Christmas, the story I was reminded of was in stark contrast.

A young man in India was given a very expensive gift by his father. The price of the particular item was $50,000 U.S. dollars at a time when the average U.S. income is $47,060 based on a forty-hour work week. In India, the average 2019 income is $2,050. Why is this story relevant? Apparently, the son did not appreciate the father's luxury gift because it was not the *right kind* of luxury gift. The son's response was to sink the new, practically perfect gift in a river.

To someone on the outside it may look as if the son "has it all." My respectful response to that comment is that no one ever in their life "has it all." We live in a world where comparisons lead us to believe that other people do "have it all." The only person in life that "has it all" is the one who has given the *illusion* to others that they have everything. No matter what you may think or feel, the grass more often than not is *not* "greener on the other side." Often times when one challenge (or several occur), our own perceived shortcomings in some areas of our lives become magnified and our minds, seeking some kind of escape, latch onto the romanticized idea that others have it so much better.

When those types of thoughts enter your mind, ask yourself: How can this be? Human beings, despite how we view ourselves, are limited. Our time is finite and just this one planet, let alone the universe, is vast. Therefore, *no one*, including royalty who have strict codes of conduct, truly "has it all."

One final thought on this matter: There is always going to be someone, somewhere, that is going to give the *appearance* that they "have it all." If that person truly "has it all," then why are they so busy trying to convince others of the fact that they "have it all?" Then again, that has everything to do with that person and nothing to do with you, unless you *choose* to let them get "inside your head" and waste your time with their nonsense. Therefore, instead of trying to "have it all," appreciate *all you have*. There is quite a difference.

~ 6 ~

TRADITION

"Tradition is a guide and not a jailer." -W. Somerset Maugham

Earlier today I went to visit my friend, Sandi, and her children, Valerie and Cameron. After visiting for a while, we went into the kitchen and mixed a combination of flour, salt, oil, and water, which was then kneaded into a malleable type of dough. At that point, we pressed the children's hands into the dough and then it was baked. Once done being baked, the molds were painted, dated and used as both decorations and keepsakes. Something so simple and inexpensive yet creative has now become a wonderful tradition while creating great memories for Sandi's children.

The current season, popularly referred to as the "holiday season," by some and the "Christmas season" by others is a time of tradition. One of the popular traditions we celebrate in my family is Philip Van Doren Stern's popular story *The Greatest Gift*, which was later adapted into the classic 1946 film *It's a Wonderful Life*. Many of the themes in that story are identical to what I am sharing with you. The only difference between *The Greatest Gift* and this book is that *The Greatest Gift* is a work of fiction.

At the current moment in time, certain traditions are often at odds with other values, beliefs, etc. I am aware this has gone on in past generations and will most likely continue into the future, long after I am gone, but it is something which is sad to contemplate.

Many cynics walk around deriding things they label as "too traditional," as if somehow tradition is antiquated and not in keeping with the popular thought(s) of the current time. Perhaps not all tradition is good and some may even have been socially appropriate at the time in which they were conceived and practiced.

However, having made the previous point, let me also state that tradition is something which links together past, present and future generations. It may be the only thing that connects you with loved ones no longer physically present or it may be the only thing you leave behind for future descendants. Traditions are a part of history, and history I would *hope* is something that *everyone* uses as a guide for the future.

~ 7 ~

INSPIRATION

"Just don't give up trying to do what you really want to do. Where there is love and inspiration, I don't think you can go wrong." -Ella Fitzgerald

Life, from the human perspective, has two sides: the wonderful, beautiful part of existence and it's dreary, soul-crushing counterpart. The fact of the matter is that the two are very much concurrent. It's what you *choose* to focus on which guides your reality. One of the *greatest* gifts in life comes in the form of inspiration.

Inspiration, when you find it, gives you a sense of drive, purpose, wonder and quite often euphoria. There are so many forms of inspiration possible that it would be impossible to list them all.

Right now, in my own life, I am feeling very inspired. It is quite an interesting statement to make because the past year in my life, and the lives of so many I love and care for, has been one of the most personally challenging and heartbreaking years I have yet to encounter.

However, through love, faith and tenacity, I have come to realize that there is truth about there being "light at the end of the tunnel." It definitely does not mean that it is easy to go through at the time. What it made me realize, however, is how very fortunate to have had and still have all that I do and all that I am in life.

As a creative-minded person, I am always hoping and praying to find something that has meaning. Deep down, any type of performer or artist who truly views the arts as a calling, longs for making meaning in their work. A life or career in any type of art can be wonderful, rewarding, or even meaningful. Again, on the flip side, it can be crushing, isolating or depressing. As important as it is to be able to express one's self artistically, there is the reality that others in many other vocations do not have to face: predictability in their profession, time with family and friends, supporting one's self financially, taking care of one's health and a million other needs.

Now, granted, inspiration obviously does *not* have to mean creatively. I used myself as an example due to the fact that I am writing a book (a creative endeavor) and my creativity and artistic side are enormously important in my life. They are in no way the sum total of who or what I am, since no one should limit themselves. However, in an attempt to tie together all of the aforementioned points previously stated, my own personal inspiration at the present time is quite high, and that is in large part due to the writing of this book. It is therapeutic in assisting me to process my own life, but the inspiration for me comes from the fact of fantasizing that it is going to help you.

I have come to realize in a world where life at times, and often for stretches, can be trite, predictable or irritating, sometimes the smallest suggestion or gesture can "light a fire" deep within and reignite one's passion. People can give this gift to other people. Therefore, why not try and find *your* passion? You never know who may be watching you.

~ 8 ~

MONEY

"Never spend your money before you have earned it." -Thomas Jefferson

Love it or hate it, money is a fact of life. It only has power because we, as human beings, choose to give it power. It is something which I can only hope imagine is limited to our existence here on Earth. Granted, there are some groups of people (isolated tribes, for example) for which money in the sense we associate does not exist.

However, very close to the beginning of our species existence until its' eventual end, money or some variation of it is going to exist. There is an old expression that it is "the root of all evil." It many ways it can be. If we pursue it for the sake of false idolism, then in leads to one of the Seven Deadly Sins: greed. If we measure another person's worth only in terms of financial wealth, then money is evil. If we commit murder or other dastardly acts over money, then it is evil. If we allow it to drive a wedge between our relationships with others, then it is evil.

A few years back my concept of money changed. I used to despise money. However, I read a book which simplified some of the lessons in *The Bible*. The section about money stated to treat it as a tool. For us to coexist in some type of organized society, taxes are unfortunately a necessary evil. *Everyone* who reaps the benefits of living in organized society needs to contribute somehow. The easiest way for that to be done is to pay money as part of said contribution. However, and this is *very* important to note, whoever is responsible for tax collection has an *obligation* to the taxpayers that the funds received are, in fact, spent in the areas for which they are allocated. Taxing people frivolously to oppress them *is* a form of evil.

Bearing in mind what we have previously discussed, the moral of Thomas Jefferson's quote is true. Like it or not, you *are* going to need money. You *should* plan for your future because at some point, you *are* going to need some of the money who have hopefully saved.

Another angle to consider in terms of money is charity. We should want to help those who are less fortunate. However, there again is an old expression that "charity begins at home." Indeed, you cannot really help anyone else if your own basic needs are not being met. You give what you are comfortably able to give. You can always tithe, if you choose, to those who have little in your last will and testament.

Remember, when you have passed on and people reflect back on your life, chances are they are *not* going to remember you by how much money you made. Therefore, if in your given vocation(s) you are voluntarily working perhaps eighty hours a week, then realize that forty-seven percent of your time, a non-replaceable commodity, is being exchanged for money, a replaceable commodity. Ask yourself if the sacrifices you are making are indeed necessary.

If you are willingly trading "big chunks" of your time to amass a large quantity of money, just realize your time on this planet *is* limited and you cannot take the money with you when you die. Therefore, treat money like a tool and focus on it when necessary.

One final thought on this topic: When balancing a checkbook, we have to look at income versus expenses so that everything balances. If your time is primarily consumed in some way concerning money, are the other areas of your life equally balanced?

~ 9 ~

ORGANIZATION

"The only difference between a mob and a trained army is organization." -Calvin Coolidge

Some may not feel the same way as me on this topic, but I *strongly* believe that to achieve a goal that you set for yourself, you have to be organized. Right off the top of my head, I can think of three vital commodities that we as a people seem to be lacking: time, money, and energy.

I realize I keep using this book as an example in many other comparisons, but I feel as if it serves to highlight different points I am trying to make. For example, writing a book of this scope and magnitude requires me to be organized. For all intent and purpose, I am attempting to create something which, to my knowledge, has never been done before.

Thus, being organized is key to my success in this endeavor. I have a list of topics written down and once I complete that topic, I scratch it off my list and begin writing my next topic. All of my handwritten notes are stored in a particular order in a folder that I keep in a specific location. I know my next step after handwriting the book will then be to type everything I have handwritten. It is a process but alas, it is an organized process.

Organization is not just something you can do for yourself. It is a vital skill that must be taught to others. Realistically, it is something that is used by society as a whole: in business, in government, in religion. You name it, really.

As a matter of fact, I can think of a great personal example concerning *lack* of organization that affected my father, my friend John and myself. We went to a concert and saw one of my all-time sources of love, hope, and inspiration: the musical band named *Earth, Wind & Fire*. I was reflecting on the experience before, during, and after the performance. Thus, if any member of *Earth, Wind & Fire* ever read this book, thank you. It is important for us as a people to let one another know how meaningful they are.

My father, John and myself were having an incredibly joyful evening, until it was time to leave. The venue where we saw the performance obviously made money their first and foremost priority. Instead of planning and *organizing* the flow of people entering and exiting the area, it was the exact opposite, a chore.

As many people do when attending some kind of event where large numbers of people are present, we waited a bit before attempting to leave and let the crowd thin. After five or ten minutes, not an unreasonable waiting time, we slowly made our way towards the exit. From that point on, we should have been outside the entire building and on the road home in no more than twenty minutes. However, due to extremely poor planning and lack of organization on behalf of the hosting venue (in a city which ironically touts itself a "tourist destination"), I ended up getting separated from the rest of the group and it took over an hour before we were finally on the road.

Thus, as a result of *someone else's* greed and lack of organization, we wasted money (on gasoline and parking), energy (trying to leave the venue), and time (due to inept "customer service"). As a result, I know that is a venue I will *never* patronize again. Their poor planning wasted three precious commodities. However, it was not a wasted experience as it was a shared memory and source of inspiration.

I hope you do value time, energy and money, to a lesser extent. If you do, remember that one of the best ways to conserve all three is to simply be organized!

~ 10 ~

SEX

"Sex is a part of nature. I go along with nature." -Marilyn Monroe

Sex has always been a part of existence. For many species (not just human), it is the way to ensure the very continuation of the species. For humans, it can be one of the greatest gifts of life, based upon love. It can also, if intentions are impure, lead to another one of the Seven Deadly Sins: lust.

Love it or hate it, sex is not going to go away. Once your brain begins producing those hormones, you suddenly start noticing others around you in ways you never had before. In many ways, sex is perhaps the main "gateway" from childhood to adulthood. Once one becomes aware of the "birds and the bees," life suddenly takes on a whole new dimension. It can feel like your world is being turned upside down.

However, interestingly enough, as much as humans talk about, laugh about and have sex, its' effects can create such a big deal, but sex usually has nothing to do with the act itself.

Anyone anywhere who is honest and who has engaged in some type of sexual behavior with another person in their life will tell you the experience was based upon their own personal perception.

At its' truest and most pure form, sex is supposed to be a physical expression of a loving bond and commitment that two people share. It is a gift for one person to completely make themself vulnerable (physically, emotionally, spiritually, and mentally). We, of course, are discussing the *ideal* form of sex, based on love and the body's natural tendency to want to procreate. However, sex is often about anything but love.

Sex is also a business, and a very profitable one: prostitution, pornography, sexual therapy, sexual "performance enhancers," etc. If used improperly, it can "chew people up and spit them out." Sex can be used as a form of blackmail, manipulation, violence, submission, depravity (Marquis de Sade *immediately* comes to mind) or motivation. Many people have been reduced to mere "sex objects" over time.

Personally, at one point in my late teens or early twenties, I was approached by a businessman about performing in pornography. Now, I want to make this clear: I was *not* seeking this type of attention. It was completely unsolicited. I suppose I fit a type of "look" that was "marketable."

The language used to describe this "opportunity" did not blatantly describe it as pornography, but I knew enough and investigated to know exactly what the offer was: travel expenses paid to a supposed exotic location for a "generous" amount of money to have a "bit of fun" in front of a group of strangers with a camera.

Now, at the time and given my age, I'm not going to lie: it was a temptation. I knew it was not going to happen, thanks to having a strong sense of self and good values, but I did picture what *could* have happened had I accepted the offer. My example brings about a larger point: many people *do* say "yes" to these types of offers.

Some of these people are able to successfully transition in other areas of life, but for many, it remains a source of shame or their personal "Scarlet letter." It really is not right and it is not fair to hold a decision like that against someone either. After all, if there was not a demand for pornography, then perhaps people would not feel the need to objectify themselves for attention and a nominal sum of money. You cannot *ever* put a price on a person's worth, dignity, or future.

With all that being said, it is very important to have a healthy attitude towards sex. When and if you *choose* to engage in a sexual relationship with someone, make sure both of your intentions are clear and the act is consensual. Please also make sure you are both mentally, physically, and emotionally mature and prepared.

~ 11 ~

CHOICES

"In the long run, we shape our lives, and we shape ourselves. The process never ends until we die. And the choices we make are ultimately our responsibility." -Eleanor Roosevelt

Life in many ways boils down to a series of choices. Do I lay in bed or get up? Do I eat soup or salad? Should I turn left, or right? Every day of our lives, we make hundreds, if not thousands of choices. As a matter of fact, we make choices so often, we probably become unaware of how often they factor into our thinking. Therefore, we could classify choices into two categories: conscious choices and unconscious choices.

Unconscious choices are the choices we do not even think about. We do them out of impulse (i.e. moving so not to be struck by a falling object, rescuing another person from some kind of danger, etc.). Unconscious decisions usually do not have any type of negative stressor associated with them since they are acted out of impulse. Conscious choices, at least for me personally, are often times more of a struggle.

At a young age, probably seventeen or eighteen where I became *aware* of the stress I was feeling, I began stressing almost obsessively about the choices I was making. Many ideas and paths seemed available to me. It was almost as if I was seeing *everything* as a "fork in the road." To me, it was a choice of making a hard left or a hard right. Crazily enough, the idea of choice to me became paralyzing. In my mind, I was associating choices (or freedoms) as limiting. How can this be?

How could such an independent, strong-minded, strong-willed person like me be questioning myself to such an extent? Maybe it was a sign of intelligence? Maybe it was rooted in self-doubt? Maybe I had heard too many stories of other people regretting their life choices? Maybe I was projecting myself too far into the future and not giving myself enough of a chance to live- make mistakes, form opinions, and grow as a person. My best guess is that it was *all of the above.*

I spoke to my father who offered me advice:

"Going in some direction is better than going in none. You can always change course." I also spoke with a psychologist.

Why am I telling you this? Life can be confusing. There is no one, anywhere, who has not doubted at least one of the choices they have made at some point in their life. (If you ever speak with someone who claims they have not, perhaps they need some kind of professional help). You see, some choices in life are not always going to be good choices. Your ability to recognize that means you possess humility about yourself and are human.

In all honesty, sometimes bad choices turn you to the good ones, the right ones. It might not always be immediate and it might not always be blatantly obvious, but when you make a choice, commit to your choice, much like an actor is told during a performance. Do not question it once you have made the decision. See it through and find out where it leads. If it does not work out, change course but do not beat yourself up.

At some point, you might even be able to look back, laugh and give advice based upon some of your weaker choices in the past. Therefore, be comfortable in your skin, ask for guidance when needed, and see what choices lead to your next adventure.

~ 12 ~

HISTORY AS A GUIDE

"History is a guide to navigation in perilous times. History is who we are and why we are the way we are." -David McCullough

Today is New Year's Eve, the last day of the twelve month, three hundred sixty-five-day year. At some point today, there are going to be celebrations all over the world to celebrate the transition of the current year to the next year. New Year's is a time of reflecting on the past and wondering what promise the future may hold. I cannot think of a more appropriate time to pause and reflect on history.

History is a vital topic and its' value is often overlooked unfortunately. It is a guide of where we have been so we may have an idea of where we may be going. Every person who ever has or ever will live is a part of human history. From the time you began reading the current page you where you are now is part of history.

Our very own DNA, which is unique to each one of us, is a history of our ancestors, our tribe. Often times in life, many of us at some point can be made to feel unimportant or somehow insignificant. Please do not *ever* feel that way about yourself and if at some point you do, consider the following thoughts.

There is a principle referred to as "Six degrees of separation." Essentially, the idea behind this principle is that every living person can be connected to any other living person through a series of six or fewer connections. For instance, you as the reader may be my friend's neighbor's son's daughter's friend's mother. Basically, we are all interconnected somehow, in some way. This brings about another interesting thought: "paying it forward," a concept I used as the basic for my book *You Never Know....* When someone "pays it forward," it means they perform three good deeds for three other people after someone has done a good deed for them. Eventually, everyone will be impacted at some point by other individuals' good deeds.

Therefore, if you are at a point in your life where you may find yourself questioning your purpose, think about history through the lens of both principles of "six degrees of separation," and "paying it forward." *It's a Wonderful Life* addresses this dilemma and puts it into perspective. Just because you may feel as if your contributions are minimal, you never know the impact you may have on others which may ultimately have a large impact on human history. That is why it is *essential* that you do your best and take it easy on yourself.

Furthermore, there is a question of

"How will history remember me?"

Often times, we do reflect on the past in some way. However, there are three important points to consider when reminiscing on the past: do not romanticize or idealize the past, do not live in the past, and do not be too critical of others in the past who have passed away. There are some obvious exceptions however. Individuals like Adolf Hitler should *never* be idolized.

Thus, use history as a guide. It exists for a reason. Extract the lessons you and others before you have uncovered. Remember also that the future is a *wonderful* thing to behold. History is not perceived as a threat because it is the known; it has already happened. The future is new, unexplored territory, just waiting for you, it's explorer, to uncover the greatness yet to be discovered.

~ 13 ~

SELF-FULFILLING PROPHET

"Whatever we expect with confidence becomes our own self-fulfilling prophecy." -Brian Tracy

Even though I have stated that my intention is to make this book a timeless experience, bear with me for a few moments now if you would. It is currently New Year's Day. The year is now 2020. (As a brief aside, there is an expression that states: "In hindsight, 20/20 (vision) is everything." It will be interesting to see how 2020 is perceived in the days to follow.) Depending upon the school of thought, it is now a new decade (some claim a decade runs from years ending in zero through nine while others believe it runs from years ending in one through zero).

Regardless of the distinction, the fact that I am part of a generation that has lived through the change of a decade, a century and a millennium is a rare experience. Time, to be discussed later, is a human concept. It does not actually exist. We as living beings use time as a tool of measurement due to finite limitations.

One of my favorite new traditions on New Year's is to experience H.G. Wells' *The Time Machine*, a story concerning the theme of time travel. It is a fascinating concept and of the many of the ideas incorporated into the story, one of the main ones is the ideal of being a self-fulfilling prophet.

Since today is New Year's Day, people all over the world are setting some type of goal for themselves. Some goals may be realistic (ex. lose weight), while others may be admittedly lofty (ex. make a large sum of money within the next six months). Many goals involve some kind of statement that involves self-improvement ("I want to be a better person," or "I want to be more charitable.") The reality is these *are* possible to achieve.

Therefore, if you want to achieve a goal for yourself, you *will* achieve that goal. The mistake that many make, however, is that it is not always realistic to achieve a goal by a specific date. That does not mean you have failed. Therefore, do not believe it for one second.

You may come up with a lofty goal for yourself this year, but may not achieve it within the three hundred sixty-five (or three hundred sixty-six days) of the given year. As you later reflect back, if you have not achieved the goal by the following New Year's Eve, will you feel as if you have failed? Suppose you do not achieve the goal you set for yourself for another seven years? You "set the wheels in motion" this year, which means you set yourself up for future success. Therefore, you did have a successful year after all.

Being a self-fulfilling prophet means one of two things:

-Mentally, you view things from a positive perspective. You say "good things are going to happen to me" and they do, in fact, happen. Or,

-Mentally, you view things from a negative perspective. You have an attitude that "it doesn't matter anyway," so why even bother? *Maybe* you get lucky and fate intervenes a bit and some unexpected miracle occurs. However, if that does not happen, then your situation is not likely to improve. I'm going to leave you with a quote to close this section:

"You can rise up from anything. You can completely recreate yourself. Nothing is permanent. You're not stuck. You have choices. You can think new thoughts. You can learn something new. You can create new habits. All that matters is that you *decide today* and *never* look back." -Author unknown

~ 14 ~

THINGS TO LOOK FORWARD TO

"It's really important to have adventures to look forward to." -John Santomas

Today, the day after New Year's Day, was my first day back to the "real world" after the Christmas holiday season. I went back to work for the first time in almost two weeks. The idea of waking up a little after six a.m. in the morning to be "greeted" by twenty-four-degree Fahrenheit weather on a January morning is *not* on my list of the "top five favorite things in the world." It never has been and probably never will be. I am pretty sure almost everyone anywhere can relate after being on a wonderful, extended vacation for an extended period of time.

While getting away from the "real world" it almost seems as if "time freezes." You get to come and go as you please, do the things you *want* to do *when* you want to do them, see the people you *want* to see, and make your own schedule. For many of us, I believe it is a form of Heaven.

However, at some point, reality comes beckoning and is a force to be reckoned with. As much as I enjoy my day job (I work in a "middle school" attended by eleven to fourteen-year old students and I enjoy *most* of my colleagues), it is still a job. I still have responsibilities. I have a schedule I must adhere to along with everyone else. By the sheer responsibility that has been entrusted in me "in loco parentis," I *have* to be a good role model for the students while simultaneously supervising, guiding, educating, and protecting them. It is *not* an easy job, but it is a rewarding one.

As much as I enjoy what I do and most of those with whom I work aside, it *is* difficult getting back to reality. I would have liked another two weeks of not going to work, but the truth is, I am actually much more fortunate then a lot of other people in other professions who do not get all of the vacation days I am fortunate enough to enjoy. What is the point of all of this babbling I am doing? It is to make a point. You *have* to give yourself things to look forward to in the future.

January, for me, has always been one of the most difficult months of the year. The Christmas season ends, the days are short, the nights are long, and the temperatures are usually cold. I am someone, although never officially diagnosed, who has what is known as "seasonal affective disorder." I could easily come home every day after work for the next two months and hibernate under my covers. I, however, choose not to do that. It is because I have too many other things I am looking forward to in the months to come.

My good friends, Jeremiah and Bridgid, are expecting a second child in about two months. I have given myself a project of going through and both organizing and donating many of my possessions. It is my hope that some of the things I have been abundantly blessed with but no longer require will help someone somewhere who is not as fortunate as me. As you know, I am *very* excited about this book. No matter how tired I am, I force myself to write a section, or chapter, a day. I dream in the coming months of sitting down in the nice, warm sunshine as I complete my first draft, which I anticipate to occur sometime in the early spring.

There are many more upcoming adventures that I am looking forward to as well. I have only mentioned some of them in this chapter. Enough about me, however. What are *you* looking forward to? Are you going through a "meh" or "bland" period of time? Life is not always going to be exhilarating.

As important as it is to live in the moment, not every moment is going to be great. Life simply does not work that way. When you maybe need a bit of excitement, try something new or exciting. It might be the start of an exciting new chapter in your life.

~ 15 ~

DO I HAVE CONTROL OVER THIS?

"You can't control the world, but when you control your thoughts, you bring order."
-Bernie Siegel

Life often times just is not fair. You are going along, day to day, trying to do your best, and some obstacle, something you have absolutely no control over, happens.

Sometimes these events are catastrophic: a loved one dies, you are in a severe accident, someone's health declines severely, you lose your job or a major source of income, you are a victim of some type of terrorist or criminal act, or, as of this current typing, a worldwide health pandemic where the world as you know it is temporarily halted. The history books will refer to this current time in history as "Coronavirus" or "COVID-19".

Often, when the "chips are down," so to speak, things sometimes get worse before they get better and can even overlap at times. It really is *not* fair. However, and this requires quite a bit of internal reflection, life is *not* fair. There are probably so many things that happen to us over the course of a lifetime that are bad that we could write a series of books. Thus, you have to make a choice: do you "throw in the towel" and resign yourself to a lifetime of wallowing in your own misery *or* do you "buckle down" and adjust your attitude?

There is a saying I saw one time that was along the lines "Life is ten percent of what happens to you and ninety percent of how you deal with it."

While it is true there is quite a lot of bullshit to deal with in this world (both circumstances AND other people), these are *not* unique to one specific generation.

These things have existed since the beginning of human existence, and will continue until our species eventual extinction.

When things really do get rough as they often do, I would strongly recommend that you ask yourself about the situation: "Do I have control over this?" If it is a situation that you do have control over the outcome, then examine why something you did affected the outcome. However, if it is something that you do not have control over, what can you do? Nothing.

We, as human beings, like to have the feeling that we are in control. It is a feeling of comfort, security, or power. As much as we like to have the feeling of control, we have considerably less than we would like to admit. The truth of the fact is that we are limited, and there is only so much we *can* control.

Probably the single biggest thing in life we have control over is ourselves. We cannot control the world, the natural order of things, or other people. Therefore, if you want some kind of positive change, then it has to begin with *you*.

You have control over how you view the things that happen to you. *You* have control over whether or not to be happy. *You* have control over the kind of person you are and how you treat others. *You* are in control of *you*. No one else. Thus, do not try to "police" other people's behavior. As a side note, there *is* a difference between condemning a behavior and a person.

When life gets hard and things outside of your control happen, you have to relinquish yourself to the outcome of the situation. *You*, however, are the only one in control of your outlook. Once you understand and truly believe that peace and healing occur within side of yourself and then hopefully you can become a guide for others also experiencing challenges.

~ 16 ~

WHO VERSUS WHAT YOU ARE

"Character is like a tree and reputation like a shadow. The shadow is what we think of it; the tree is the real thing." -Abraham Lincoln

When we are young, we are often asked the question:

"What would you like to be when you grow up?"

Being young and idealistic, there are so many dreams that we envision for ourselves. Sometimes we follow these dreams and actually become what we aspire to be. Others of us stumble along the way and take a bit of time to "test the waters" and see what feels right for us. While it is important to know what we want to become, the question we should truly be asking is:

"*Who* do you want to become?"

While vocation is very important as we all have to find something to contribute, a niche, the type of person one is in life speaks volumes. To be brutally blunt, not everyone can be a politician or "world leader." Honestly, at least from my perspective at the current point in world history, the people *most* deserving of leadership roles do not want them, and the people that deserve them the *least* want them the most.

We, as humans, often look at these people and idealize them in a way. They become some false icon with more power than any one person should *ever* have. Again, it is very important to note that these people only have power because other people *choose* to give them power.

Therefore, it is very important to look at a person in a position of power through a "lens" of constructive criticism. I observe these "idols" that other people idealize and they often possess the "what" it is that people obsess over, but I am much more concerned with the "who" these people are. The "image" someone projects of themself is irrelevant, but what truly matters is the content of their character.

Many people earn a reputation for themselves in their given professions for their dedication, innovation, and drive. However, what does any of that even mean if a person undermined, undercut, or manipulated other people that get into that position? True, the person achieved the "what" they desired, but they sacrificed something much more essential along the way: the "who," their character.

While it is true that every job in the world is not inspiring or glamorous (the grass is *not* "always greener on the other side"), someone *needs* to do some of these jobs. Regardless of how you may feel, you *are* contributing something and you *are* being self-sufficient, both of which are crucial to humans.

At the very end of your life here on Earth, people might reflect back on your profession. That most likely is *not* how you are going to be remembered though. You will be remembered for the type of person you were, how you impacted others through your deeds, and the natural talents and abilities you possessed that made you unique and how they impacted your personality.

The stark reality of the world is that when it comes down to a job, or vocation, or whatever other name you may choose, there is always going to be someone else to fill the void for that particular job. The job itself is not unique, but *you* are. Therefore, put your focus into *who* you are, not *what* you are.

~ 17 ~

DISTRACTIONS

"By prevailing over all obstacles and distractions, one may unfailingly arrive at his chosen goal or destination." -Christopher Columbus

I believe that one of the biggest obstacles that prevents us from reaching our true potential (and hindering happiness) is distractions. Often times distractions lead to procrastination which leads to goals not being met which leads to unhappiness (or unfulfillment). It is a chain reaction, so to speak. Now, I am not saying that all distractions are bad. Sometimes they are needed. They can cause us to have "tunnel vision," which can prevent us from "seeing the big picture." They can also be useful in self-preservation so we do not consistently focus on negative thoughts and feelings. However, like pretty much everything else in life, distractions should be limited in *moderation*.

We live in a world that is full of distractions, perhaps more now at the present time of this writing than at any other time in history. Will that change? I honestly do not know because I have no way of knowing what the future holds. The very essence of being a human being though means there are going to be distractions. On a planet currently with a population of seven plus billion people, how could there not be distractions?

As much as I would love to be able to fully commit myself to the writing of this book, it simply is not possible. My life has many demands and distractions which require me to give attention to other areas of my life as well. My specific choice of words on the page demand that my mind is not "wandering" as I focus on my goal. Personally, in many areas of my life, I have to force myself to remain motivated.

I have many goals for myself in life that I hope to one day achieve. Often times I find myself *thinking* about the things I would like to achieve and then I get exhausted thinking about them. I often fall asleep.

For example, earlier today I fell asleep three times before sitting down and forcing myself to go downstairs and write. I knew that in order to achieve my daily goal, I had to change my behavior otherwise I would continue to distract myself and procrastinate.

Often times, I think people have many ambitions. They become distracted and then lose track of time needed to take the physical actions necessary to achieve whatever those ambitions may be.

As wonderful as the *idea* of being able to magically manifest our thoughts into actual existence, the idea is pure fantasy. I happen to believe it is a wonderful fantasy, but the reality of the situation is that is a fantasy nonetheless.

Therefore, bear in mind that while distractions at times can be good *and* necessary at times, at some point you have to stop living within the parameters of said distractions and start taking concrete steps towards some goal or ambition, no matter how big or small it may be. Then, when you reflect back, you can feel good about yourself when you think:

"I really did that, didn't I?" When ambitions become reality, it creates a strong sense of pride and accomplishment. Those are two of the greatest feelings one can experience.

~ 18 ~

LEARNING TO SAY "NO"

"The art of leadership is saying no, not saying yes. It is very easy to say yes." -Tony Blair

Often times people think saying "no" is the same as being difficult or not being able to "do it all." Granted, it can be both of those things and sometimes is necessary to respond "no." "No" is the fastest way to communicate to someone that something is simply not going to happen.

There is a common phrase which has been around for years which is the idea of being a "yes man," out in the workforce where there is *no* (ironic use of the word) request made by a boss or supervisor of some kind that an employee will decline. It is often times associated with yet another common workplace phrase:

"I don't want problems, just solutions."

Well, guess what? Perhaps that boss or supervisor should *not* be in a leadership role. Perhaps these people need to be told more often,

"With all due respect, but *no*, that is *not* a reasonable request." *No one* is above reproach, regardless of what they might *think* of themselves.

The truth of the matter is that there are a million and one reasons that you could be told "no" by someone else, and a reason is not always necessary in every circumstance. Thus, do not feel guilty every time you do say "no," especially if you are justified in your reasoning.

Somehow saying "no" has come to be viewed through the years as being obstinate, not being a "team player," mean, rude, or somehow incapable. This is now going to bring us back to the point I made earlier about not being able to "do it all."

"Yes" can be very dangerous to respond to every request made of you if you do so indiscriminately. You could potentially be overextending yourself, making empty promises you cannot fulfill (which could damage your reputation), put you in danger, or cause you to compromise your sense of morality among many other unrelated consequences.

Each and every person has a sense of free will. As a result, we each individually have our own ways and choices of what we will or will not do. Not every request or question that you get asked is going to be reasonable, regardless of who is asking the question. Do not hesitate to say "no" if you feel strongly about it or have your reasons.

Granted, some people might simply say "no" because they do not like someone, and that is okay too. No one is "universally popular." Everyone is going to encounter critics in life.

33

Some people, usually ones in actual or perceived positions of power, however, view "no" as a challenge to their ego. Guess what? That is too bad. You do, however, have to consider possible consequences for yourself in these types of situations when you respond "no" to a superior on the job.

I personally though am a strong-willed individual and am becoming more "confident in my own skin" as I grow older. Thus, when I say "no," I mean it and am willing to deal with the consequences if necessary.

There is an expression:

"Say what you mean, and mean what you say."

When you say "yes" and "no" when you actually mean it. Ultimately, people *will* come to respect you for having principles, even if they do not always agree or understand your reasoning.

~ 19 ~

LISTEN, AND DO NOT SPEAK

"Wisdom is the reward you get for a lifetime of listening when you'd have preferred to talk." -Doug Larson

Listening is one of the simplest things in the world a person can do, but few often stop long enough to engage. People want to be heard. Often times, there are a variety of excuses why we *cannot* listen.

"I'm busy" or

"I have something/somewhere I need to be/be doing."

Granted, there are those amongst us who do not have the ability to physically hear. Maybe you, the reader, are one of those people. Perhaps you have some type of other impairment that does not allow you the traditional use of your ears. That is much different than what I am discussing here. I am talking about the state of *active* listening.

The definition of listening I am referring to could be defined as "the ability to accurately receive and interpret messages in the communication process." Each and every one of us have ways of conveying our thoughts, feelings and emotions. There are many examples that come to mind of ways we communicate: speaking, Sign Language, laughing, crying, singing, writing, and many more.

Nature and the world around us have a way of communicating with us humans too. Birds chirping, dogs barking, the wind howling, the Earth quaking, the sun shining, and snow blowing are examples of this phenomenon. How often do *you* actually stop to listen?

People too sometimes take what is known as a "vow of silence." Often times, vows of silence are associated with spirituality or deep reflective thinking.

Why is listening so important? For beginners, it shows someone that you care. Many people, especially those among us of an advanced age, often times get lonely, especially if their loved ones have passed away. Older people often possess much wisdom on a variety of topics.

At one point in time, elders were revered and treasured for their lessons of wisdom. Sadly, during my time, I am noticing a trend of younger generations not holding their elders in the same high esteem as they once were. However, I am very hopeful that this unfortunate trend will reverse itself and go back to the way it used to be and still *should* be.

At the current time in which I live, information is available from a wide variety of sources. As a result, people's natural ways of receiving information is rapidly changing. Many people are therefore "cutting themselves off" from other people via artificial means while still having access to various means of information: reading, listening, or watching.

However, and I cannot stress this enough, there is a *big* difference between researching a topic, time, or way of life and *listening* to someone who actively lived or experienced those events firsthand.

Therefore, if you are "busy running around" day to day, "going through the motions," try something a little different and actively listen to the world around you. Listening reminds each and every one of us of our interconnectedness and helps to deepen our own humanity. Just remember that as much as *you* want to be heard, others want to be heard as well.

~ 20 ~

RESPONSIBILITY

"The price of greatness is responsibility." -Winston Churchill

Humans cherish the idea of freedom. Freedom is the will we have to make our own choices. With choices come actions, and with actions come responsibility. This *should* be obvious, but for some reason, it is perhaps the single biggest dilemma facing humans.

You see, the problem is that when someone makes a choice that is *beneficial* to them, that person wants to accept the consequences of that choice. However, when someone makes a choice that has unintended consequences, many people often times attempt to deflect responsibility or even try to "shift blame" on other people for their own failure(s). No one should do that, ever. Do not make excuses.

Many of the problems that the world faces could be alleviated if everyone worried about themselves and accepted the consequences for *all* of their choices. It is incredibly easy to sit back and critique something else that someone else does. It is *not* very easy to take personal ownership.

At the time in which I live, there are many people who are manipulated by other people, usually government "officials" and "world leaders," into thinking that they are "victims" of circumstance, and therefore not responsible for their own actions. Not only is such a message condescending, it is downright dangerous. As a result of this type of thinking, many individuals no longer have a sense of personal responsibility unless it is personally beneficial. Any type of negative consequences suddenly become "society's problem." With that type of thinking, nothing will ever get resolved, only worsen.

Now, and this is also very important to understand, sometimes it is an individual's responsibility to step in and prevent another person from making a harmful or dangerous choice that could negative affect that person or other people. In that specific circumstance, the responsibility *should* be to protect and nurture.

There is a reason why children need to learn about responsibility. It is also the same reason at times the elderly or other individuals who may be incapacitated in some way need to be guided. They may not understand or foresee possible consequences of their choices.

For example, a few days ago my father's personal property was accidentally damaged by someone else. At the current time, it is an exception for someone to accept responsibility for an accident in which there are no witnesses. The woman who had the accident made the right choice by accepting responsibility for her actions, which is commendable.

It is not easy to say: "I messed up." The truth is, *everyone* messes up sometimes. Personal responsibility is very important. Freedom is not something which is truly free. Despite what moral relativity may dictate, the choice is simple: all actions have consequences. The path to self-improvement and discovery begins with *you*.

~ 21 ~

PATIENCE

"Genius is eternal patience." -Michelangelo

Patience is one of the most important qualities to possess in life, yet there seems to be such a short supply. It is not something that can be bought, taught or acquired. Yet it is something that is fundamental and in order to achieve, it is something we *all* must demonstrate at some point in our lives.

I can think of some great quotes related to patience:

"Don't wish your life away,"

"Rome wasn't built in a week,"

and "Patience is a virtue" immediately come to mind. Quotations are a great insight into the fact that you are *not* the first to think or feel certain ways about topics nor will you be the last. Often times, there is a great amount of insight and wisdom in others' thoughts and quotes.

Why is patience so important? Well, to put it bluntly: life is not predictable or linear. It can "throw curveballs" at you and therefore often times does not follow a set of rules. As much as you might like to try, you cannot really schedule or plan life.

In a way, life would be ideal if it were similar to the scientific method: there would be dependent variables (of your choice and which you could control) and the independent variables. The problem is, there are so many variables which occur during the course of a typical day that it can be easy to find yourself thinking:

"Oh, it's ten a.m. I cannot wait until three p.m. so I can leave and go home." What is the problem with that type of thinking?

Well, you are "wishing away" five hours of your life that you are never going to get back (time *is* a commodity). You may even be totally justified in wanting to go home. Maybe whatever it is you are doing for the next five hours is unpleasant, uncomfortable, or boring. Thus, the times in life that are *not* great make you enjoy the times that *are.*

Why are we discussing patience? The culture and world as I know them at this time in many ways are obsessed with what is "new" and "upcoming." While there is nothing necessarily wrong with that type of thinking, doing it all of the time can really present some problems. It creates unrealistic expectations of immediate gratification for everything, and that is truly unhealthy.

The fact of the matter is that life is often periods of waiting. Sometimes the waiting can feel unbearable. Yet, as my father says to me:

"Where there is no choice, there is no conflict."

Since each and every one of us are mortal beings, you would think everyone would be more comfortable with the concept of patience. If we cannot change time or control many circumstances, why "stress out" over such matters?

The simple fact of the matter is that many events in life will "fall into place" and happen when, how and how they are supposed to happen with or without our intervention. Thus, perhaps each of us should demonstrate a bit more patience with others, the world around us, and ourselves. Therefore, we may truly get the most out of each moment. Carpe diem.

~ 22 ~

PERSPECTIVE

"I believe everyone should have a broad perspective of how the universe operates and our place in it. It is a basic human desire. And it also puts our worries in perspective." -Stephen Hawking

I have been spending quite a lot of time recently contemplating a perspective on life. The writing of this book has really affected me in a positive way, both through daily interactions and advice I am offering when asked. I have so many thoughts and ideas that I want to share. Obviously, not each and every one of them can make it into this book.

One of the things I have found myself doing is much self-reflection. Various events happen, sometimes to us or others or everyone (the 2020 COVID-19 outbreak is currently occurring), which cause us to reflect on the past. Other times, there are many signs and coincidences which occur that can cause one to question: what is the meaning of this? It is *too* coincidental.

One such example is very fresh in my mind. I happened to be thinking about old neighbors of mine and discussing them recently. At this point in time, I have been out of contact with them for almost ten years.

About an hour ago, I happened to be reading the local newspaper. An article about an area family's home burning down caught my attention. As I read the article, would you believe it was my old neighbor's house?

To say that I am a bit stunned by this coincidence would be quite an understatement. The story ties together so many of the points about life I am attempting to make in this book: interconnectedness, signs from the universe/coincidence, the importance of family and joy of giving.

The surrounding community raised quite a bit of money for the family whose home was completely destroyed. However, perhaps the most important elements to emphasis from the story are people and hope. The way one views such matters is from a particular perspective.

You see, the longer you live in the world, the more life experiences you personally encounter. There are some days it does not seem possible that I have seen, heard, or lived, whether directly or indirectly, through all that I have in the relatively short period I have been alive.

At times, life can feel like an extreme ride, perhaps a roller coaster. When it really gets crazy, it is essential to step back and put things into perspective. In other words, be in the "here and now."

From personal experience, one of the best ways to acquire perspective is to meditate. There are a variety of ways to meditate, but it usually involves some kind of deep reflective thinking within one's self, either alone or in a quiet, relaxed environment, where you are very aware of your immediate sensory input.

Your perspective on things may be your single most important guide in your journey through life. The older you get, the more things *change*, and the more they change, the more they stay the same.

One word that describes life is "dichotomy." As strange as that is to read, it makes sense through the lens of existence. Much of our time here is strange and foreign. That is okay. If we are honest, I think every person has felt that way at some point. Just always remember, your perspective and relationships with others *will* guide you in the right direction, but *only* if you allow yourself to be open to the possibilities.

~ 23 ~

HAVING IT "YOUR WAY"

"There's a way to do it better-find it." -Thomas Edison

I am one of the first people to admit that I like to do things "my way." Whenever I hear the song *My Way* by Frank Sinatra, I can absolutely relate. Ever since I can remember, I have had what could be referred to as an "independent streak." Often times, I know exactly what I do or do not want or know how I do or do not feel. Are you the same way? Be careful, this can lead to another one of the Seven Deadly Sins: pride.

My mother often tells me a story of when I was one week old and I started holding my breath until I turned blue. I had learned at a week old to throw a temper tantrum because I was not getting what I wanted (in this case, to be held). A year or two later, when I first began talking, one of my first responses to either a question or command was: "Don't want to."

As you can imagine, I put both of my parents "through the ringer" in many ways during my formative years. I was born, after all, under the Zodiac sign of "Scorpio," and Scorpios are known to be very strong-willed people. As I have gotten older, however, I have consciously tried to tone down my assertiveness, which is not always easy.

We live in a world that seems to want to celebrate our uniqueness. We hear phrases such as:

"You do you,"

"Have it your way,"

and "If it feels good, do it." While these messages can be good, are they good if we follow these mantras all of the time?

Sometimes you *cannot* have things your way. Sometimes you *do not* have a choice. In a world where billions of people inhabit, it *is not* always about you, nor should it be. At one point in time, countries closer to the western hemisphere had a reputation for being more individualistic, where more emphasis was placed on the individual.

At the same time, countries closer to the eastern hemisphere had a reputation for being more collectivistic, where emphasis was placed more on society as a whole. Through the years, a mindset similar to "we are one world" has taken hold (reference "globalism" for this idea).

Customs, cultures, and ways of thinking and feeling have changed. By and large, one way of thinking (collectivistic versus individualistic) has taken hold. Guess which one? As a result, more people have become much more self-consumed and narcissistic than ever before.

Now, let me take a time moment to pause and state that there are many wonderful people who are *not* narcissistic, but enough that it is indeed a problem. Thus, it is very important to address the importance of it *not* always being about you, the individual.

Is it sometimes important in life to have it "your way?" Absolutely. There are going to be times where you have to have things your way, especially if they pertain in some way to safety, your morality, or even your own individuality (*not* going along with the rest of the crowd just because it is the "popular" thing to do).

One thing to remember, however, is that you cannot always have it your way. Sometimes compromise or sacrifice is done out of necessity. Bearing that thought in mind, you try to do your best, and I will try to do mine.

~ 24 ~

DOING IT ALL

"It's not about doing it all. It's about doing your best at all you can do." -Author unknown

I got home a little while ago from doing some promotional work for a show I am on called *Herrings*. I am very fortunate to get to work on the show as an actor with other artists. I realize the word "artist" can come across as being pretentious, and quite frankly at times it is a bit of a cliché. However, I am *very* lucky to get to work with this wonderful group of people who also happen to be very talented, which does *not* always happen in show business.

You're probably wondering:

"Why is he mentioning this and what does this have to do with 'having in all?'"

Well, I am using show business as an example here because as much as I love the "show" part, I hate the "business" end. At the end of the day, it is a business like any other and so when the group gets together to do something work-related, it is only natural that the topic of other "gigs" come up or other projects one may happen to be working on at the time. The reality of show business is that it can be long, grueling hours with intense bursts of work and then several hours of downtime. During said downtime, various conversations can, and do, take place.

During my downtime this morning, several of us were sitting around waiting for the hair and makeup to be done before stepping in front of the camera. I proudly announced to everyone how important this book is as a creative endeavor for me. Naturally, when one talks about something as broad and massive in scope as a timeless book about life, people have plenty of suggestions. I invited everyone to give input for the book at that point.

Now, here is where I am going to "tie" the discussion at hand back to the topic of this section: having it all. While we were having the discussions about "the business" this morning, it made me think of "doing it all."

As I have stated many times already, I *love* performing. It is one of my biggest passions in life and I cannot imagine my life *not* being creative. However, performing can also become addictive, cause one's ego to become enlarged, and narrow one's perspective.

Show business has its' own mantra:

"You're only as good as your next job."

As a result, it can be a gypsy-like existence at times. The amount of work that any working professional in the business does happen to land, prepare, and keep (if lucky) before moving onto their next job is "mind boggling."

It is very much a study in numbers, having a large "network" of people to maintain relationships with, "selling yourself" (like it or not), and consistently acquire and/or maintain new or existing skills. At times, it *can* feel as if you are "doing it all."

No one, anywhere, can "do it all" or "have it all," and if you try, there is a strong possibility at some point that you may have a physical or mental breakdown (or both). At the current point in time, the culture is trying to make people feel as if they can "do it all," and if they cannot, they are somehow inadequate. That is a toxic mindset and I hope you do not fall prey to that dangerous way of thinking.

Regardless of what you may have been led to believe, no one anywhere has, or can, "do it all." Other people may try to sell you on the *illusion* that it is possible, but it really is not. Anytime you commit yourself to one area in life, another area is neglected.

Therefore, you really have to be honest with yourself and prioritize what is important to you and what is not. Sometimes you need to give yourself a break. I know I, for one, by my own personal standards have been giving myself a bit of a break and guess what? *It's one of the best decisions I have ever made.*

~ 25 ~

AMBITION

"He who blinded by ambition, raises himself to a position whence he cannot mount higher, must thereafter fall with the greatest loss." -Machiavelli

Ambition is very important. Ambition, together with drive, is what helps you to accomplish, or achieve in life. However, and this is very important to note, *blind* ambition can be downright dangerous.

Ambition, in its' best and purest form means that you care and have passion in your life. Maybe it makes you want to better yourself in some way. Maybe it causes you to want to help and improve others' situation(s). In these particular instances, I believe your ambition to be good, or pure.

Blind ambition, on the other hand, can cause a series of problems. Many times, ambition forms from a genuine feeling of wanting to achieve something great. However, depending upon the goal and the obstacles in the way of achieving said goal, one can form "tunnel vision." "Tunnel vision" is no good if a person loses sight of all else in the world around them.

It can also lead to other negative behaviors to achieve that goal: narcissism, double-crossing, and betrayal, just to name a few. I also feel as if another point needs to be addressed while discussing ambition: nepotism.

Many people do not like to acknowledge nepotism, but it would be naïve to suggest it does not exist in the world. Who, at some point in their life, has not benefitted in some small way, from happening to know someone in a particular situation that they used to their advantage?

Nepotism is part of human nature. Why would you not help someone you know, like, love or care about? Many people, but not all, who go on to achieve large levels of success in particular field(s) have benefitted by being connected to the right person(s) who provided them with an opportunity. Granted, the person perhaps had to prove themself, but the fact remains they were given a chance.

Ambition is a part of one's personality. Often times, people become aware of an opportunity and they begin campaigning for said opportunity, often times to embarrassing levels.

As an aside, I am going to pause and personally admit I am *not* a fan of awards or recognition for a job well done unless it is for truly an outstanding accomplishment (saving a person's life, for example). Many times, awards often seem to be based on ego, campaigning and nepotism.

Occasionally they are based on merit for exceptional performance in a given field, but often times they promote unhealthy levels of competition and more emphasis is placed on the award itself than the satisfaction of a job well done. Doing one's best should *always* cause the sense of fulfillment and perhaps after a lifetime of exceptional work than recognize someone. Other than that, a simple "job well done" as well as adequate financial compensation in the workplace should be thanks enough.

In closing, ambition (in moderation) is great. It can absolutely help lead you on the path of self-fulfillment. Just remember to keep your ambitions "in check" and never lose sight of who you are or what you will or will not do to achieve said ambitions.

~ 26 ~

WHAT YOU HAVE

"Do what you can, with what you have, where you are." -Theodore Roosevelt

Unfortunately, often times the world seems to promote superficial ideals. Many people fall victim to the idea that someone else, somewhere else, has something better. There are quotes that support this theory:

"Bigger is better" and

"Keeping up with the Joneses" immediately come to mind. Basically, it boils down to this simple, toxic idea:

You are in some way inadequate because you are not or do not have (insert your own idea here).

Essentially, at its' simplest form, this is competition. Someone else has "planted" the idea in your mind that in some way you do not "measure up."

There are two possible motivations that come to mind: someone is attempting to project their own insecurities onto you or, most likely, someone wants your money.

At the current point in time, many people in the United States live way outside their means. As a result, several years back, many were approved for loans they had no way of *ever* paying back. Thus, the country was thrust into a recession. Worse yet, many of those same people never learned the lesson and are *yet again* living in homes not appropriate for their income level and household size, own one (or several vehicles) completely unnecessary for their needs, and spend money faster than they can generate. Again, many of these same people have little to no savings (or "rainy day" funds), and only view things in terms of immediate gratification. In other words, people are focused on what they do not have, not on what they do have.

The sad reality is that people that live in the aforementioned way often spend so much time working to pay off their frivolous excesses that they lose much time with loved ones. Why? I will personally never understand that type of thinking.

My best guess, however, is that in their mind they are either:

1.) Competing with someone else.

2.) Trying to fill some kind of void in their life

3.) The powerful business forces in this world successfully brainwashed people into thinking they need these material goods.

Once one starts losing sight of what they do have, many negative qualities become apparent. Often times, the simplest and most important joys in life become meaningless, feelings of restlessness can occur, and even detachment from reality happens. What is the true cost?

You cannot put a monetary price on life. As previously stated, one comes into this world with nothing and leaves with nothing, except the life they lived. Life has a much deeper meaning than who has the newest (insert whatever is the "must have" of the current moment in time).

If your "must have" in life (besides the essentials needed to survive) is something *other* than people, other living beings and your own personal views on faith or a deeper meaning or higher power(s), then I respectfully suggest that maybe you reexamine your priorities. Things are replaceable. People are not.

~ 27 ~

PLEASING EVERYONE

"Care about what other people think and you will always be their prisoner." -Lao Tzu

In my experience, one of the biggest challenges many people face in their life is worrying about what other people think. I am acutely aware of this fact due to my background working in education. Day in and day out, it feels as if I am saying to a student:

"Don't worry about what _____ thinks. You worry about you." My colleague Karen also is constantly telling the students:

"Stay in your own lane."

Why is it so difficult a concept to grasp? I understand it is a lot more difficult as a young person to be independent as often times one is more impressionable and trying to find one's place in the world. However, as an adult?

With all due respect, unless you are *directly* responsible for assisting me or giving me something, I could not give two _____ about your opinion. I would hope you feel the same.

Now, what I am going to say is yet another one of life's dichotomies: do not be someone that is a "professional agitator" and goes out of your way to tell people that you do not care about them or their opinion. Additionally, that extends to being intentionally offensive or spiteful. That is just being a jerk, pure and simple.

Instead, be comfortable enough in your own skin to "march to the beat of your own drum." Do not conform just to appease other people. However, some people do once again take this idea to the extreme just to refer to themselves as "non-conformists." The irony is that many of these "non-conformists" often share the same "rules" or ideas they are "rebelling" against and, as a result, ending up conforming to "non-conformity."

In many ways, the current time in the world is bizarre in many ways and people selectively pick and choose which societal "rules" apply to whom and in what circumstance. These "rules" are constantly changing and are *completely* subjective.

Yet, enough people seem to buy into said "rules" that if someone *dares* question any group or "movement" that views themselves as the "enforcers" of these "rules," then that person is a (insert adjective with a negative connotation(s)).

In my view, anyone that thinks or acts in a dismissive manner towards another person or group or even *attempts* to characterize other people in such a negative, stereotypical fashion is, at the very least, a sycophant and at the very worst, dangerous.

The simple fact of the matter is that actions speak louder than words. Words *do* matter, but way too often people know how to speak well, but then do *nothing* to back up their thoughts or ideas. "Group think," which has become all too common, limits free speech and free exchange of ideas. "Group think" is akin to lemmings jumping off of a cliff together.

Therefore, *do not* worry about what other people think. As I previously stated, each and every single one of us is on our own unique path in this life. If someone tries to intimidate you into thinking, feeling or acting like them, that is because *they* are weak-willed and absolutely powerless without followers. To quote the singer Dolly Parton:

"Find out who you are and do it on purpose." Lead by example, and others will at the very least respect you for remaining true to your convictions.

~ 28 ~

LISTEN TO YOUR INSTINCTS

"Be a good animal, true to your animal instincts." -D.H. Lawrence

Each and every one of us has instincts or "gut feelings" about situations, people, etc. The older you get, the more you realize just how vital it is to actually *listen* to these instincts. I could list many examples of times I have listened to my instincts as well as times I have not, but I am going to share one instance as a child where I did listen to my instincts that may have very well saved my life.

One evening, when I was about ten or eleven, I was walking by myself to my friends' house, a few blocks from where I lived at the time. My parents had already had the necessary talk that *every* parent needs to have with their child(ren) about "stranger danger." Thus, I always had a heightened sense of awareness of my surroundings. That evening, as I was walking, a vehicle abruptly pulled to the side of the road next to where I was walking.

Since this happened quite unexpectedly, I glanced inside at the driver. A balding, middle-aged man with glasses leered back at me. I would go so far as to say this person was looking *through* me. Every part of my body let me know I was in immediate danger and to walk as far away from the vehicle in the opposite direction as possible.

I quickly moved and as soon as I did, the vehicle raced away in the opposite direction. There is no doubt in my mind whatsoever that this person had evil, devious intentions on his mind and that I unfortunately found myself in his crosshairs for a brief period. Luckily for me, I listened to that feeling deep down inside myself and let it guide me out of a potentially dangerous, if not tragic, situation.

How many times in your life do you or have you gotten frustrated with yourself for either not listening to your gut instinct or second guessing your first reaction to something to later find out your original response was correct? I think everyone has done that at least once in their life.

D.H. Lawrence made an interesting observation with the quote I used to open this section. Human beings are a supposedly "evolved" species capable of critical thought and more complex actions. Nevertheless, species other than humans use their instincts to survive. If instincts are supposed to guide and protect us, then why do we often question those instincts? The answer to that question is free will.

Humans are aware of the basics needed to survive: air, food, water, and shelter. Throw in relationships with other people and their surrounding environment, egos, and "higher level thinking," and suddenly something which is simple becomes much more complicated.

One point I will make is this: Roughly ninety-five percent of the time your initial gut feeling or reaction to a situation I going to be the correct one. Stop second-guessing yourself. You can learn *a lot* from observing a "man's best friend": a dog.

Dogs love humans in almost all cases unconditionally and often times are more loyal and love humans better than dogs do themselves. Yet dogs live according to their instincts and usually have a very good "read" on people. Kind of makes you wonder about how "evolved" we humans supposedly are, does it not?

~ 29 ~

REDEMPTION

"No human being is so bad as to be beyond redemption." -Mahatma Gandhi

Many times, the world can be unforgiving. Someone somewhere makes a mistake and immediately a critic is there to point out said mistake. Unfortunately, due to advancements in technology, many people's past mistakes have been recorded in some form so future generations have access to what may be someone's personal low point in life.

Now, before what I say here is taken out of context, some people's deeds *need* to be made available at times for either public safety or history lessons. However, on the same token, if someone does something wrong in the past but they are truly sorry and regretful of their action(s), they too deserve a chance at redemption.

I am not going to lie. Some people do some truly horrible things in their lives which can have catastrophic effects on other people. I personally have known and experienced these feelings from *both* sides. When these events occur, they have a tendency to "shake you to the core," and can cause one to question their faith, if they have any. That being said, *intent* means quite a lot as do circumstances and time. People can and *do* change. No one stays *exactly* the same as they once were.

Let us make an assumption about someone who makes a terrible mistake. For example, let us use someone who is a drug addict. Suppose the drug addict kills someone while under the influence of drugs. (All too often this is a reality.) The addict *did not intend* to kill someone, but it happened nonetheless. What happens if that event causes the drug addict to quit drugs?

Granted, the innocent person who was killed is gone and cannot be brought back. They were truly a victim of someone else's choice(s). I can virtually guarantee you that *if* the recovering addict has a conscience, they are going to regret killing someone every single day of their life.

Many people in this situation would demand retribution, the idea of an "eye for an eye." However, the victim is still not going to be brought back. What does retribution accomplish? It is a cycle of intense negativity that holds back everyone affected by the situation.

Therefore, if the addict has faith or belief in redemption, the "silver lining" to be found *could be* if that person shares their experience and prevents at least one other person from making a similar disastrous choice(s). (I realize this example is *very* sensitive and please know if you have ever been on either side, my prayers are with you. Drugs are truly evil and turn people away from their good, natural natures).

Remember, *everyone* makes mistakes in their lives. Some people's mistakes are much more disastrous than others. What matters the most though, is if one is truly sorry and wants to redeem themselves in some way. One of the hardest things as a person is not to judge other people. However, how do *you* feel when you find yourself on the receiving end? Good people do sometimes make bad choices, but they deserve a second chance.

~ 30 ~

IS THIS WORTH STRESSING OVER?

"It's not stress that kills us, it is our reaction to it." -Hans Selye

Stress, whether you like it or not, is *not* going away. It is a part of the human condition. Our bodies naturally produce stress as a reaction to the world around us. However, not all stress is bad.

Stress is generally broken into two categories: eustress (positive) and distress (negative). Some stress is outside of our control, while other stress is internal (self-imposed).

If you allow it, eustress can be a positive motivator in your life and can enable you to achieve some great accomplishments. Distress, on the other hand, if remained unchecked, can compromise your immune system and potentially kill you. It is *that* powerful.

Right now, I am going to focus on distress. Why do we allow this type of stress to affect us in this manner? We are literally allowing ourselves to be destroyed by something we *do* have control over.

I am very familiar with distress because I let it wreak havoc on me for years. As I get older, I am getting better at managing the stress. I have a tendency to focus on *what could go wrong* instead of focusing on *what could go* right, a literal shift in thinking.

Over the years, any time I am feeling distressed, I have taught myself a variety of "tricks" to divert my attention away from said stress: force myself to smile, tell a joke, exercise, write, laugh or help someone else, to name a few. After dealing with distress for a long enough period of time and working myself into both a state of disgust and exhaustion, I find myself asking:

"Is this worth stressing over?"

Much of the stress we face in life is indeed self-imposed. A thought as simple as:

"Things *have* to be this way or _____," is going to cause you stress. Life does *not* follow a designated set of rules, as much as we would like. There are many, if not most, situations in life where we do *not* have control. The thing we *do* have control over is how we *choose to react.*

If we *choose* to be very rigid and exercise as much of our personal will as possible, things are more likely to be stressful (distress). If we *choose* to take a more "laid back" and carefree approach to things, they are likely to be less stressful.

It is not possible to eliminate all of the distress in life. However, you *can* make efforts to minimize its' impact on you by figuring out how to react in the healthiest way for yourself in unpleasant situations and to shift your way of thinking. Talking and being honest with your-self and others can also be incredibly therapeutic.

I know for me, personally, writing has always been a way for me to relieve negative stress. It is very cathartic and leads to moments of clarity. I always hope that when I commit some of my thoughts to a page that someone, somewhere, who is maybe going through trying times, may read something that I have written and realize they are not alone. It is a very freeing feel-ing to realize that you *do* have the power to help someone else.

As you move along your journey, you are going to find that often times your biggest weak-nesses ironically enough can become, or highlight, your biggest strengths. To reiterate once again, always remember you > stress.

~ 31 ~

BE TRUE TO YOURSELF

"Sometimes, being true to yourself means changing your mind. Self changes, and you follow." -Vera Nazarian

I cannot stress the importance of this enough, but more than anything in your life: be true to yourself. The world is a very big place and often times life is "dog eat dog" type mentality. At the current point in world history, which I sincerely hope changes, freedom of thought, communication and the free exchange of ideas without retribution is under attack.

Not only is this *undemocratic*, but it is downright dangerous. I personally find it nauseating how many people mindlessly follow the crowd. There are *way* too many followers and not nearly enough *true leaders*. Often times, the "leaders" of these large groups are false icons and have their own narcissistic, twisted worldview as their guide.

I apologize if I am sounding a bit cynical. I, by my nature, am not a cynical person, but sometimes in life to address certain issues you have to remove your "rose colored glasses" and face issues head on.

I realize this has been stated previously, but each and every person is a unique being. There has never been one of *you* before and there never will be another *you.* Yet time and again I see, hear and experience how people are treated like pieces of personal property, if not worse. I do not know how you feel about this, but I find it to be absolutely *disgusting.*

You are *not* a number. You are *not* a demographic. You are *not* a statistic. You are a thinking, feeling, living being with contributions to make to the world.

There have been times in my life where I have been in relationships with other people that made me realize I was compromising my own autonomy. Guess what? That is *not* okay. That is what is known as a "toxic relationship." Anyone that truly cares about who *you* are is not going to have conditions about what *they* expect from you, nor should you of them. They take *you* as *you* are.

I now, at this point in my life, am the most comfortable I have ever been in my own skin. As a result, I am becoming much more discerning what *I do and do not want to do*, whether it be situations, relationships with other people, or any other area which may be applicable.

Now, when I say:

"No thank you," it means

"No thank you." I have processed the information and have no desire at all to do whatever it is I was asked to which I responded:

"No thank you."

I am not sure what your philosophical beliefs about why you are here or what the meaning of your life may be. I *can* tell you from experience that standing up for your beliefs, speaking your mind, and staying true to your convictions make you unique. There are going to be times when it is going to be challenging. Other people may even try to "break" you, but that is because they perceive you as a threat and means that you maintain the power. Do not waiver.

Life is tough enough to live by following the natural rules of nature without worrying about whatever some dolt follower or "leader" is trying to "sell you." Find *your* inner voice and "to thine own self be true."

~ 32 ~

EXPECTATIONS

"No one's life ever goes as they planned. That truth alone should bring a sense of relief to everyone." -Andrena Sawyer

I am going to share a bit of news with you here which is not exactly "Earth shattering": things do not always go according to plan. I know, it is not fair. Guess what? Say it with me:

"Life is not fair." Since that is not something any one of us can change, you might as well adjust your thinking.

I realize this is a topic and recurring idea through the book, but I do believe it cannot be emphasized enough. As much as humans like to think we are in control, we are not. We are a limited species and all of us have an expiration date. There are so many unforeseen variables in life that we either take for granted or of which we are completely unaware, there is absolutely no way we can take all of them into account when we plan.

Now, if you are a believer in fate, chance, something higher, or all of the above like me, then it makes it easier to accept when things *do not* go according to plan. You might say to yourself:

"There is some reason that did not happen," or

"Sometimes a door closes so a window can open." We do not know how or why these things happen, and I do not think we are supposed to know or understand them.

There is a saying along the lines of:

"Hope for the best, expect the worst, and be prepared for anything." My grandmother, who had the most wisdom and insight of anyone I have ever met in my life, always used to say to me:

"Blessed are they who expect nothing, for they will not be disappointed."

Since life if very unpredictable, I think the best piece of advice I can give you is this: take things at face value and do not be locked into a certain type of thinking. For example,

"It has to be this way or _____."

You can, and should, plan for the future, but take into account that things change, times change, and *we* change. At times it is easier to "go with the flow." Do not be so hung up on the idea of what you want. Be more concerned with who you are.

As I am sure many of us have learned along the way on this journey we call "life," there are so many unforeseen experiences which happen, *no one* could have foretold them. We might like to try and plan our life in a way and "map it out" something similar to a linear line in math, but at the end when we look back, our line is anything but linear.

Along the way, there are going to be some truly wonderful experiences and people and, on the flip side, there is going to be the exact opposite. Some of these things are going to pull us in all kinds of directions and cause us to deviate from our "plan." Guess what? It happens. That is life. Each and every one of us have that common shared experience. It is the basis for the phrase:

"The best laid plans."

Therefore, why fight that which you have no control?

To close off my thoughts for this section, I would say when you have expectations, keep them broad. Realize a million things that you could never anticipate may happen in between the vision in your head of what *could* be and the actual reality of what *will* be. Be realistic with yourself and about the world around you. Finally, remember that no matter what happens, you are strong enough to handle whatever may come your way, and it is a part of your own unique story.

~ 33 ~

KEEP MOVING!

"The life of a man consists not in seeing visions and in dreaming dreams, but in active charity and in willing service." -Henry Wadsworth Longfellow

Being an active and contributing member of society is essential for each and every person in life. Not only can laziness be detrimental to one's health, but it can also pave the way for another one of the Seven Deadly Sins: sloth.

If you research history and the evolution of human existence, you will note how our ancestors had to do *everything*: cook, clean, build, hunt, etc. They were forced to use their bodies and their brains out of necessity. Thinking back to the sketches depicting the evolution of our species, humans have become less, for a lack of a better term, "ape like" over time and are one of the rare mammals of the homo erectus type.

As you may have guessed, we are *not* designed to be sedentary creatures. However, laziness/inactivity have become *enormous* problems through the years, leading to a rise in a variety of negative outcomes: mortality, obesity, health issues, skyrocketing medical costs, economic issues, and limited personal and professional output. In a way, and this is very sad to admit, laziness is causing the human species to *devolve* and is one of the likely causes of our eventual extinction, unless changed.

Now, I am not suggesting that you need to be busy doing something every minute of the week. In fact, just the opposite is true. Sometimes you have to slow down and take a break. However, taking a break is very different from stopping completely. No one can dictate to you to do better, especially if what you are giving is your personal best. You know when you are achieving your maximum potential and when you are not.

However, I have noticed a trend over the past number of years. At the current point in time, the more artificial "advancements" created by humans, the more apathetic and lazy people have become. Thus, many people are less inclined to go outside, socialize, even use their own voices to speak. All of this most likely "boils down" to technology. The most alarming of all is those who allow their technological devices do their thinking for them.

I predict technology is something that will last or, at the very least, have a large impact on humans for the next few generations until there is the next "big breakthrough" for our species, whatever that may be.

It is important to note, however, that the aspects of laziness and apathy have increased with humans' discovery of ways to make life easier. While that notion in and of itself is a good thing, you still have to use your brain and body. There never has been nor ever will be a substitution for a human being.

The secret to a meaningful existence is to get out and do something with yourself. Only you know what you can and cannot do. Only you can limit yourself and your potential. Regardless of what you have been led to believe, things in life are generally *not* handed to you on a "silver platter." You have to work for them and when you do put in the actual work and effort, you have the feeling of having accomplished something. When we sit down and look back, would you not like to have a long list of accomplishments rather than a list of what might have been?

~ 34 ~

TIME IS A COMMODITY

"Lost time is never found again." -Benjamin Franklin

Time is a commodity. Yet, for something which is so precious, why do we waste so much time? Suppose you live to be exactly eighty years old. If you live exactly eighty years, that is 29,220 days or 42,076,800 minutes. That might sound like a lot, but is it really? There are a lot of different ways you could divide into these numbers, but one thing is certain: time is something you really should not waste. Allow me to give you an example.

This morning, for whatever reason, my alarm did not go off for the time I had set it for. Has that ever happened to you? I know it is a feeling I *hate*. By the time I did get up on my own, I was approximately behind schedule by forty-five minutes. Starting off my day that way is not something I enjoy. I prefer to give myself a "buffer" of time between when I wake up and when I leave in the morning.

However, since I was running late, I did not have that buffer. No matter what I did from the point at which I woke up, there was literally nothing I could do to get back those forty-five minutes. How often has a chunk of time gotten away from you?

Let me provide you with another example. Let us say you "kill time" doing something meaningless three times a week for an average of thirty minutes per activity. That is ninety minutes a week multiplied by fifty-two weeks a year for a total of four thousand six hundred eighty minutes. Now, let us once again take that even further and say you "kill time" at this rate for sixty years. 4,680 multiplied by sixty equals 280,800 minutes of your life spent "killing time." Now, to tie this idea back to the person that lives for eighty years, if they wasted 280,800 minutes of their life, they wasted more than 1/200 of their time here on Earth. Does that put things into perspective a bit?

Yes, I realize time can "get away" from all of us at times. You are not going to be able to use every minute you have doing something of your choosing. However, being *aware* of how you spend your time can be enormously beneficial.

A lot of times it seems many people are in denial about death. Yet, it is a fact of life and something each and every one of us is inevitably going to experience. Death itself should not be obsessed over, but I believe that having a realization that it is a part of the cycle of life and has a definite bearing on the preciousness of the time we *do* have should hopefully make everyone "wake up" and realize that the time we are given matters.

There *is* going to be a point where all of us are referenced in the past tense. We all will, at one point, be of another time. Therefore, since time, to quote The Steve Miller Band, "keeps on slippin, slippin, slippin into the future," make the most of the present. The past is the past and soon enough the future will be the present. I am going to close out this section with a quote, which ties it all together perfectly:

"Yesterday is history, tomorrow's a mystery, that's why today's the present."

~ 35 ~

DREAMS

"Every great dream begins with a dreamer. Always remember, you have within you the strength, the patience, and the passion to reach for the stars to change the world." -Harriet Tubman

Let us be honest, shall we? Dreams are wonderful. Fantasizing about something is about the most blissful thing I can imagine that must exist for someone. It, to me, is about as close to Heaven as one here on Earth can get without actually being in Heaven. All of those "feel good" chemicals secreted by our brains give us a feeling of utter joy (euphoria).

Earlier this evening, I received validation in the form of a letter that I am closer to achieving one of my dreams. The letter confirmed I am now eligible to join one of the largest unions in the world for film actors, known at this time as "SAG-AFTRA."

I know I have already stated I am an actor. The entertainment industry is one of the most notoriously difficult industries in the world given its' nature, and many actors view just the invitation to join the union as a "rite of passage. For me personally, the eight-year path has been long and arduous and I am *very* proud of the fact that I have *earned* the recognition to be accepted into a chosen vocation. Does the letter itself necessarily mean anything? No, but it is a milestone to me that one of the goals (dreams) I have set for myself is one step closer to becoming a reality. I hope my personal example is motivation for you to work towards something *you* want.

Now, what of *your* dreams? Dreams are absolutely fantastic, but the reality to bear in mind is that even if some of your dreams do come true, very seldom is the reality of the situation the same as what you envisioned in your mind.

Often times, what we do not realize when we dream is the amount of work it is going to take to accomplish. Many times, in addition to work, there is a lot of sacrifice and time commitment required. Sometimes, you may achieve said dream and at that point no longer want or care about it. Finally, to reiterate once again, there is also the possibility of reality not meeting your expectations.

Sometimes, dreams do not work out. How many people fantasized about being able to fly like a bird as a child? Perhaps you envisioned yourself morphing into some type of mystical creature. Granted, maybe you do not mind now, but often times what we spend so much time fantasizing about as children is later replaced by the facts of life.

Perhaps this is why we value childhood so much? It is equated with dreaming, where anything seems possible and where we have not yet been jaded by real life? Whatever the case, do *not* stop dreaming and do *not* stop believing.

Have faith in yourself to realize that if can think of it, it probably can be done. If you are starting to question or be "hard on yourself" because it feels like your dreams are not "panning out," look around at some of the absurd inventions or ideas created by people through the years and remember that somehow those ideas became a reality, so why not yours?

Those people had drive and tenacity to get their ideas realized. Just ask yourself which of your dreams means the most to you and what steps, sacrifices and amount of time you are willing to trade to pursue your dream(s)?

~ 36 ~

IMPORTANCE OF ALONE TIME

"I have to be alone very often. I'd be quite happy if I spent from Saturday night until Monday morning alone in my apartment. That's how I refuel." -Audrey Hepburn

Some people cannot stand to be alone but others love solitude. A lot of people, I think, fear being alone because maybe deep down there is something they do not like about themselves. Robin Williams once observed:

"I used to think the worst thing in the world was being alone. Now I realize it is being with people who make you feel alone." Huge difference. As much as I enjoy being around people at times, there are other times I absolutely cannot stand the thought of being around strangers.

Last night, for example, I got very little sleep and as a result have been extra irritable today. As a result, I have been trying to limit my social interactions. To make matters worse, on my commute to and from work, I observed other people being more aggressive than usual and getting into other people's "personal bubble." Then, as I left work today, a student walked right into me and said absolutely nothing.

Now, I realize I have been practicing mindfulness and controlling my own reactions to situations I cannot control. Since I am feeling irritable and people were bothering me so much, I decided to forego one of my favorite activities after work: going to my local gymnasium.

I, like many people, try to improve my overall health by getting in a good workout at the gym. Most days after the workout I feel invigorated. However, there are other members at the gym that do not practice the concept of "personal space" and sharing with others. Some days, I simply cannot bear the thought of tolerating that type of behavior, so I therefore give myself a break.

It is better to "check" yourself and realize:

"I cannot handle this right now."

I think way too often people keep on pushing themselves until something inside "snaps" and they take out their frustrations on other people. There is nothing wrong with giving yourself and others a break sometimes. Some days you simply need to give your brain, body, and spirit a chance to recharge. Sometimes, you might even need to be alone for more than a day.

Society over the years has somehow arrived at the conclusion that it is important to "be where the action is," when in fact, often times the exact opposite is true. We all need to be left alone with our thoughts and feelings at times, if for no other reason than to reflect.

Sometimes to figure out what you truly want requires alone time. The action of me writing this book requires me isolating myself for a period of time. I get very annoyed if something comes between me and my writing. How would I accomplish my goal if I did not give myself the alone time that I require? The answer is simple: it would not happen.

The next time you feel like you need a break, take one even if you just give yourself five minutes of quiet time. We all need time to ourselves just for moments of clarity or to "reset" our ways of thinking or feeling. Even if other people do not like you taking a break, that is their problem. At least one person is happy: you.

~ 37 ~

LIVING IN THE PRESENT

"If you want to be happy, do not dwell in the past, do not worry about the future, focus on living fully in the present." -Roy T. Bennett

You may view the concepts of "time as a commodity" and "living in the present" as the same. While I agree there are many parallels and overlapping ideas, let me explain why they are different.

Viewing time as a commodity is an action that one takes so the day does not pass them by. It is a realization that you are never going to be able to recapture the current moment in time. Now, living in the present refers to psychologically investing yourself in whatever is going on at a particular moment in time. It is almost as if you allow your senses to provide sensory input which is providing "snapshots" of wherever you may be.

There is a phrase about people sometimes going on "auto pilot." This phenomenon essentially states that although someone is physically present, they are mentally "going through the motions," but in fact may be mentally "checked out." Now, stop and think for a moment about one of the defining moments of your life.

You probably can recall the date, time, weather, sights, sounds, smells and the way you felt. Whatever the particular event I just described may have been for you personally, that was being fully invested in that particular moment. Now, the point that I am making is to try and have as many moments like that as possible.

I realize not everything is going to be memorable nor is it going to be pleasant. However, if you are experiencing one of those moments in life as you read this, what are you thinking? What are you feeling? Is it possible there may be a lesson to be discovered in whatever the situation may be? If you are currently being "put through the wringer," compare whatever negative feelings you have with a moment of pure bliss in your life. Pause for a few moments.

Now, realize that if things are bad, they are not *always* going to be bad. Life is cyclical and very much a journey. Even though you may want to run away or somehow escape from the current moment in time, realize that in doing so you are attempting to rush away a part of your life.

Living in the present or "being in the moment" is something that I think each and every person struggles with at some point. We live in a world that seems to be obsessed with "progress" and "what's next." While that type of thinking or questioning is not necessarily bad in and of itself, it does take the focus off of right now, the present. Therefore, perhaps everyone needs to slow down a bit.

Perhaps we should live our lives as if we are devouring our favorite food. Instead of quickly devouring whatever might be on our plate, instead take the time to let each morsel dissolve at its' own pace on the tip of our tongue. Since our time on this planet is relatively limited, maybe we should all sit back a bit more and just marvel at the fact of being.

There are so many unsolved questions just on *this* one planet. Where do you fit in? Where do I fit in? How do we all fit in and fit together? If you are not taking the time to slow down and be in the "here and now," life *will* pass you by. You could potentially be missing out on so many truly wonderful moments if you are not taking the time to truly appreciate them. Therefore, why not wake up and "smell the roses" before it is too late?

~ 38 ~

PRACTICALITY

"Without vision you don't see, and without practicality the bills don't get paid." -Paul Engle

Being practical or having a sense of practicality is an *essential* life skill. Practicality brings with it order, common sense, and realistic ideals. At the current moment in time, there are so many *impractical* things taking place throughout the world, only chaos emerges from these situations.

I am going to use myself as a personal example. I have many goals I have set for myself. I like to think I am doing a pretty decent job of finding a balance and accomplishing the steps needed to ultimately achieve these goals. Now, herein the lies the struggle for me personally.

I believe I have stated that I am a driven person and that I really do not like to say "no" to someone I care about or admire out of fear of disappointment. Often times I am asked to participate in events. I am always very flattered that someone either thinks highly of me personally, my talents, or both.

The reality of the situation, however, is that many times I do not say:

"No thank you" to an opportunity that presents itself and instead I find myself saying:

"Yes, sure." Since I often tend to "bite off more than I can chew," I either end up becoming exhausted, sick, or both. Does this sound familiar to you as well?

The truth of the matter in this situation is that when I say "yes" too often, I am being *impractical.* Even though there is a part of my mind that absolutely wants to "do it all," the reality is that often times my body is not up for the challenge.

There is an unwritten rule in life that to do something well means you can really only focus on one thing at a time. Anyone who attempts to challenge this rule is sooner or later going to be limited or incapacitated at some point.

As I sit here and write, I cannot help but think of a family friend, Michael. He was loyal, intelligent, funny, and generous to a fault. Michael, who was Jewish, used to get more excited about Christmas than people that celebrate the holiday. He was also very, very driven.

Unfortunately, Michael had a "friend" that lived with him, but did not work. As a result, Michael, out of his own generous and good nature, supported both he and the "friend." Michael also had the thought in his head that he, like his father, was going to die by the age of forty-seven.

Michael worked and worked, often in excess of one hundred hours a week. Everyone around him who actually cared about him said,

"Michael, slow down. You're pushing yourself way too hard. Take it easy on yourself and kick out _____ ("friend")." Michael would not listen. Eventually, he *did* push himself too hard and needlessly passed away shortly after his forty-seventh birthday.

I discuss Michael with my parents sometimes. He was a truly wonderful person and is very missed. Yet, he ultimately became a self-fulfilling prophet. He died at a young age because he was told himself he was going to die at a young age. He ignored his sense of practicality by not listening to his body even though it gave him warning signs to slow down. As a result, the world lost a loving, unique person *way* too soon.

If any of what you just read sounds familiar, do something to change the pattern of behavior. Each and every one of us has to be practical to reach our happiest, truest potential.

~ 39 ~

ATTITUDE OF GRATITUDE

"An attitude of gratitude brings great things." -Yogi Bhajan

Before I begin this section, I have a few thoughts about current events which I am going to use to connect to the main idea. Right before I sat down to begin writing today, I happened to read the news. A local man who would go onto become internationally famous for his basketball skills was killed in an accident.

The man, Kobe Bryant, was only forty-one. Making the situation colossally worse, his thirteen-year old daughter, her thirteen-year old friend, and several other people were also killed in the accident. Something so horrific is unfathomable. Some things in life cannot and will not ever make sense. They are beyond our abilities to comprehend. I cannot even begin how all of the victims' families are going to have to endure their losses and the intense coverage of the story due to Kobe Bryant's fame.

Many people truly appreciate all that they have in life: loved ones, health, status and possibly material wealth. Some people, however, seem to focus on what they do *not* have, but would love to possess. These same people do not appreciate all that is good in their life.

As all of us *should* be aware that life can change in an instant. I am going to defer back to my example of Kobe Bryant. From the "outside looking in," he "had it all": family, money, fame, extreme success in his given field, and admiration to name a few. However, his fate and that of several others, including two young girls, has been forever altered in the blink of an eye.

It should not need to be stated but let me remind you: *life is precious.* Our time here on this planet can and will come to an end at some point. Do not walk around with a "chip on your shoulder" like you are "owed" something by other people. Live and let live so to speak.

Do not focus on all that is wrong, focus on all that is right. Do not focus on what you do not have. Instead focus on what you do have. There is a lot you are going to experience during your life, either directly or indirectly, and much of it may cause you to have more questions than answers. That is normal. That is a large part of the human experience.

Be thankful for the simple fact that you even became a person at all. Out of the hundreds of millions of sperm deposited by your father and the countless eggs released by your mother, that one unique conception led to you. Each and every one of us is a literal miracle.

Therefore, do not walk around sulking all of the time. If you feel down, try taking a walk outside and taking in all of the splendor around you. Look at some of the people in this world that are remarkable or admired. What about them makes them remarkable? What traits or qualities do they possess and display that makes them special? What similar qualities do you possess that could make you a similar type person?

The truth is none of us are stagnant. We are all capable of change if and when we want to change. Since life is so short and unpredictable, change your attitude for the better immediately. If you are already an upbeat person, thank you and continue to lead the way.

~ 40 ~

IMMORTALITY

"Millions long for immortality who don't know what to do with themselves on a rainy Sunday afternoon." -Susan Ertz

In the current time in which I live, many discuss the concept of immortality. What exactly are they referring to, however? At this point in time, immortality can be defined as "living forever." How can this be? No human being can live forever.

Immorality, I think, is something that people associate with other concepts, namely a belief in the afterlife and the legacy one leaves behind in this world, usually after having achieved a certain level of fame.

For argument's sake, however, take the idea of immortality and divorce the meaning of this word from those other concepts. It is not possible for *any* person to be an immortal being, save for Jesus Christ, who was God in human form. Yet, when someone dies, people often say:

"Their legend lives on," or something similar.

While it is true that a person's memory or legacy lives on, the person themself has ceased to be in this life. It is theorized that human civilization is about six thousand years old, which may *sound* like a lot until you realize that Earth, at the *minimum*, is millions of years old. By that comparison, humans are a mere "blip on the radar."

What is it about our species that makes us think we are so unique? Once again, let us tie the concept of humanity to immortality. Why do humans think that we are capable to live on through the ages? Does anyone recall dinosaurs? Granted, they were another species and perhaps did not have the same reasoning capacity as humans, but if they *did*, do you think they would have thought they were going to exist forever?

I am not attempting to belittle the accomplishments of the human species. In fact, I think just the opposite. I am in awe of what we have managed to accomplish in a relatively short period of time. However, the one thing I *do* find dismaying is how arrogant the species has become at believing we have "conquered" so much when, in reality, we probably have not even "scratched the surface."

The idea of someone living on through the deep, meaningful life they led is something each and every person *should* strive for. *How* each individual achieves something that outlives them is a matter of both what they do and who they are. You may very well leave behind a rich legacy or wonderful memories to be passed down through the generations.

The one idea we need to let go of as humans is immortality. The simple fact of the matter is that at some point humankind is going to come to an end. It is not a question of *if*, but instead of *when* and *how*. Therefore, the very notion of immortality itself becomes neutralized by the eventual end of the human species. It is a very deep and philosophical type of thinking, but also one that in fact references immortality. *If* you do use that term, immortality, are you referring to it in *this* life or *another* life? They are very different.

~ 41 ~

RELATIONSHIPS

"I don't need anyone to rectify my existence. The most profound relationship we will ever have is the one with ourselves." -Shirley MacLaine

One of the key parts of a person's life at some point is their relationships with others. These relationships can be with blood relative(s), friend(s), partner(s), colleagues, neighbors, acquaintances, etc. The list is endless. While it is true that no person is an "island unto themself," it is also true that some relationships simply are not meant to be.

The sad and unfortunate reality is that many of the people in this world do not like the people with whom they happen to share a bloodline. Stop and think for a minute. Are any of us given the choice of who, what, when, why or how we were born? We were placed into this world without the luxury of choosing our families.

Now, since each of us is unique, naturally everyone is not going to get along with our other family members. There are a variety of personalities, relationships, past histories, and perceptions that come into play. Sometimes too, some family members can create some type of issue ("drama") or heartache that causes a rift in the family.

It is very sad and unfortunate when these situations arise and since we all only have one "blood family," it is for the best to try and extend an "olive branch" if things get rough. As long as you know you tried, it is up to other members of the family to work on themselves. If nothing else, at least you tried.

When the relationships involve friends, it is much easier because you get to choose them. Many times, in this life your friends are more loved and confided in than your blood family. The number of friends you have is irrelevant. It is said if you have one true friend in this life, then you are incredibly fortunate.

As for relationships with significant others/partners, I do think it is important for everyone to have at least one true romantic relationship in life, but the fact of the matter is that these types of relationships are not always going to be the romanticized "happy endings" that so many fantasize about.

Romantic relationships take time, effort, sacrifice and often money to have a chance. A few months ago, I ended a relationship with someone. For a while, I had on my "blinders" and was infatuated with this person. There were many warning signs which I foolishly ignored and naively told myself:

"Oh, that behavior will change" or

"That is in the past."

I began making many choices and compromises I did not want to make, and it began negatively affecting me physically, emotionally, and mentally. At that point, I had to be honest with myself and say:

"This is not working. I cannot imagine a future with _____, nor do I want to."

It had become a "toxic relationship" and I was losing sight of myself due to the fact that I thought I was in "love." Looking back, I may have been in love with the idea of being in love, which can be very dangerous.

Since that relationship is so fresh in my mind at this time (and gave me much of the insight into writing this book), let me tell you this: if you are in a toxic relationship with someone, ask yourself if the cost of that relationship is really that important to you or other important people in your life, especially if there are children involved. They come first. It might take a little (or a lot) of "soul searching," but if you decide the cost is not worth it, do yourself a favor and walk away. The truly important relationships in your life should not take that much work and you always need to consider self-preservation.

~ 42 ~

QUALITY VERSUS QUANTITY

"People that aren't used to quality always choose quantity." -Author unknown

The topic of "quality versus quantity" permeates so many different areas of life, among them time and material goods. In both cases, a lot of times the phrases "less is more," or conversely "bigger is better" are used. Which is the more important mantra?

This is truly a philosophical question. I was reminded of this earlier this evening while viewing one of my favorite shows. The show, *The Good Doctor*, had a character facing a terminal illness diagnosis and he no longer wished to continue his treatments. It was at the point whether the quantity of his remaining time versus the quality was brought into question. Far too often, many people are unfortunately faced with the same question due to their own health issues. It is a perfectly valid question.

With anything in life, the debate usually boils down to which is more important: quality or quantity? Well, when one discusses quality, I personally frame it as the value of something (good or bad) whereas the quantity is the measurement of the amount (high or low).

For instance, is it better to have a closet full of low cost, cheaply made clothing which will only last a year or two or a closet full of more expensive, finely stitched garments that will last several years? This is an opinion question, and your answer might vary over time. When I was younger, I know I would have wanted something lower cost while having a higher quantity. Now I have come to intensely dislike shopping and appreciate having fewer things, so I would be willing to pay a bit more.

Another example to consider is the number of years someone lives. I have known many people (too many) over the years that I loved and cared for that were diagnosed with an illness of some kind. Often times, the disease was in the later stages and prolonged treatment may have extended their lifespan by a few years. However, this of course begged the question:

"Is living to eighty instead of seventy-five worth it if many of those days would mean extreme discomfort, excessive exhaustion, and multiple trips to the doctor(s)?"

Is that quality? Is it worth those five extra years? Again, these are deeply personal and difficult philosophical questions to consider.

Here are some possible questions to consider in these types of situations:

-What is your age?

-Does it involve children?

-If you are the primary breadwinner, who then will be the provider?

I know for me, personally, over the years and having seen and experienced quite a lot, I have come to the conclusion that when it involves me, I will choose quality over quantity. I believe so many times in life I was brainwashed into thinking that just because there is more of something means that it is better. I do not believe that to be true anymore.

I like to think of food when having the "quantity versus quality" discussion. Think of the most delicious food you can. Which is usually better tasting: the larger or the smaller portion? Again, to me the smaller-sized portion tastes better because the flavor is more concentrated. Quality versus quantity is not an easy subject to discuss nor is it one everyone will see "eye to eye" on. However, I hope my perspective on this topic may give you a new way of viewing that you may not have considered before.

~ 43 ~

ALL GOOD THINGS MUST COME TO AN END

"All good things must come to an end." -Geoffrey Chaucer

The aforementioned quote has been around for centuries. In my experience, it seems that so many of the good things in life not only come to an end, but they go much too quickly.

An immediate personal example that comes to mind for me is the completion of this book. I began writing on December 21. It is now January 30. I have written every day. I remember when I first began my writing how exhilarating a feeling it was to have something new and creative in my life. Now, some forty days later, I am probably halfway through this endeavor.

Granted, I am still going to have to type (I write longhand first and then scribe my work), but a big chunk of my "brainchild" is that much closer to completion. What about you? I am sure you probably feel the same when it is time to end some pleasant period in your life. It is not fun and sometimes it is much harder to do than other times.

My father retired from his job almost three months ago and he still has not grown accustomed to the idea. It is a strange notion. One works for years at one job/career. Once that person reaches a certain age, achieves a certain personal savings goal, or begins experiencing health issues, they stop working.

Perhaps "stop working" is not the right phrase because does anyone ever "stop working?" Let me put it this way: They stop performing specific duties for an individual(s) at a specific time(s) for which they are financially compensated. How does that sound?

Retirement is truly a bizarre notion. Many people I know who have retired say it is nothing like they anticipated. They expected to "settle" into the idea of living on their own terms, but in its' own unique and perhaps ironic way, work was one of the "...good things that must come to an end."

The very idea of good things coming to an end is not something unique to any one individual. I saw an estimate a day or so ago of the number of people that have existed since the beginning of time until the present (as January 2020). The estimated number is one hundred eight billion. Can you fathom that? One hundred eight billion unique stories and experiences, but yet each and every one of them has or will experience the "changing of the tides."

Not every second of every day of your life is going to be great. Honestly, life is a strange mixture of so many different things it probably would be impossible to define. However, when things are good, "milk" the most out of every moment that you possibly can.

When things are merely "meh" or even bad, try to find something in whatever situation you are in that you might find amusing. I personally laugh many times each day. My sense of humor is vital to me and is one of the qualities about myself that I treasure the most.

I understand if you may be of a more serious nature and perhaps humor is not as easy for you as it is for me. In that case, find something around you to take in, focus on, and simply appreciate. Even if things are "meh" or bad in the present, as we previously stated that "all good things must come to an end," I would also respectfully counter with the idea that "all bad things must come to an end as well."

~ 44 ~

POPULAR CULTURE

"Excellence in obscurity is better than mediocrity in the spotlight." -Matshona Dhliwayo

Tonight seems like a good time to write a section on popular culture, which I am "clumping" together with fame and popularity since they are interconnected. Why am I writing about it now? The timing seems to be very appropriate. You see, the previous few weeks and the next few weeks are popular times for shows which are going to be produced for large audiences.

Large numbers of people discuss these events as if they have some bearing on reality when the truth of the matter is that these are groups of vastly overpaid individuals giving themselves a "pat on the back" for doing their jobs in front of a global audience. What is the allure?

Well, many of these events are driven primarily by revenue and advertisements. Many people have been duped into giving billions of dollars to make already wealthy people even wealthier, while other people throughout the world are literally starving to death. Why? Many of these people want to "have a piece of the action," or to experience some of the "glamour," "fame," or "exposure" associated with these events.

Again though, why do these events hold any significance in the first place? The answer is quite simple: other people decide who and/or what is relevant and choose to give power, fame, and money due to some perceived "special quality" that someone is believed to possess.

In the current time in which I live (the United States of America in 2020), the culture is dangerously dictated by the popular "fads" at the present time. Some individuals with absolutely no discernable talent(s) become "famous" for inexplicable reasons. Once the culture has decided these same people are no longer "relevant," they are discarded like yesterday's trash. What does this say about the culture?

Let me be the first to say I cannot even really begin to imagine how a subject as vapid as "popular culture" holds such significance. Furthermore, I can only hope that the future generations place more emphasis on the betterment of humankind and use many of the mistakes currently being made as future history lessons.

Being "popular" is not necessarily as great as it seems. People might like you because of who they *think* you are as a person, but you have to question whether or not they have ulterior motives. You also have to question that if a person is popular and suddenly stopped being popular, would others still be interested in that person?

At the present, way too many people are into "fads," many of which are dangerous if not downright deadly. For example, in the middle of a global pandemic right now at which there is not a known cure for the coronavirus, which is highly contagious and people are supposed to be remaining as quarantined as possible, some people think they are being "funny" by literally licking doorknobs and public toilets since it is taboo. See the "humor" in those examples? Me neither.

These same people are literally willing to say or do anything for attention. The culture has unfortunately become that depraved. Many of these same people take their own natural talents, which make them unique, and waste them just to fit in with the "in crowd." They often times have a very bleak view of the future and their worldview is defined by the current "fad" of the moment. It is a depressing observation of the current reality. However, I can only hope and pray that by the time you read this, much of what I have written about is exactly where it belongs: buried in the past.

.

~ 45 ~

FAMILY/FRIENDS

"Family and friendships are two of the greatest facilitators of happiness." -John C. Maxwell

Today is my parents' wedding anniversary. Thirty-four years ago today they said "I do" to each other and thus began a lifetime partnership. Both of them have been through *a lot* together over the years, good and bad times, but the important thing is that both of them have "stuck it out" and grown together. I am incredibly blessed to have been given Charles and Lisa as my parents in this life. I would not have wanted it any other way.

How about you? How is your relationship with your family and friends? Your "family" is not always necessarily a blood relation. Anyone who truly loves you for *you*, they accept you and love you unconditionally for the simple fact that you exist, these are the *most* important people in your life and you need to let them know how much they mean to you as well.

The term "friend" is often used much too casually. A true "friend" is someone that would literally give you the shirt off their back, someone you could say *anything* to and they would still be there for you, or someone who will be there in your darkest hour(s), regardless of when or where, and would not care about any "inconvenience" for them. I hope that you have at least one person like this in your life.

Think of all of the traits I have just described in family and true friends. Have you ever experienced situations similar to the ones that I just described? If so, were these people there to support you in meaningful ways? If yes, then that is wonderful. If not (unless they themselves had some overlapping extenuating circumstances as well), perhaps these "family" or "friends" are neither and are mere acquaintances.

There is nothing wrong with acquaintances. Usually they are friendly enough to hold a conversation with or perhaps participate in some type of mutual activity, but usually everything with these people is "surface level." When "push comes to shove," they are not the people you first call upon (and vice versa) when things are bad.

You might see these people at some point, but that is not guaranteed. Alas, they are acquaintances and not friends, which are not the same at all. There is nothing wrong with being discerning in your language about this either.

The world at times can be a mean, cold place. The most important people in your life are the ones that make it much happier, that much more bearable for you. You are never going to find anyone as loyal or unconditionally loving in this world, ever.

Therefore, make sure you spend enough quality time with the people you love since no one is going to be around forever. Do not waste your time trying to impress people you might think are important, but realistically could care less about you.

It is also important that you be careful about who you let into your "inner circle" of family and friends. Should a new person be introduced into the group and suddenly there is some "drama" or "issues" that did not exist before that person, take it is as a sign that the problem is with that one person and not the rest of the group. Always remember: Your family and friends love you and knew you "back when." They are not replaceable.

~ 46 ~

HEALTH

"To keep the body in good health is a duty...otherwise we shall not be able to keep our mind strong and clear." -Buddha

Your overall health-mind, body, and spirit- is essential. Yet many times people do not take the necessary precautions to ensure theirs, or others' health or only worry about their health when they are *not* healthy. Why?

Many people treat their bodies like machines: they keep pushing themselves until something eventually breaks down. They very real fact is that no one is invincible. Last night, for example, my father was walking down a flight of stairs after leaving one of our favorite restaurants. It was a bit slippery out and the area was not well-lit as it should have been.

While walking down the stairs, he mistook the next to last step and fell pretty hard onto the ground. Thank God, he did not hit his head or any other vital body part. Aside from some bumps and bruises, he was otherwise okay. Yet, it served as a reminder of what could have happened.

Earlier today I stopped at the store to buy a few items for my mother who has been sick for the past few days. There have been many stories in the news about communicable diseases. While I was shopping, I repeatedly kept passing this person who was violently coughing, and not making any attempt to cover his mouth so as to prevent any of his germs from being spread. I immediately started thinking to myself:

"What is that guy spreading through the air that other people might catch?"

It is absolutely *disgusting* and *everyone needs to cover their mouth with their elbow or a tissue* whenever possible while coughing or sneezing.

I have been discussing physical health. Now let us take time to discuss the importance both mental and spiritual health as well. Unfortunately, for many years, mental health issues had a stigma attached to them that if someone had a mental health issue(s), then that person was "weak" or "nuts." That is an absurd and downright dangerous way of thinking and feeling.

Our brains are a part of our bodies just as much as any other part of our body. They are very complex organs, yet we still know relatively little of them. However, they are essential to who we are and cannot diminish their importance.

The matter of the fact is that many, if not most, people in one way or another have something wrong with their brain chemistry. If this is you or someone you know, it is *okay*. You are not alone. Just like you would go to see a cardiologist if you were having problems with your heart or an ophthalmologist for problems with your eyes, you go to see a psychologist or psychiatrist (or both) for an issue with your brain. There is absolutely no shame in that whatsoever.

Finally, your spiritual health is essential. Without going too deeply into the concept here, make sure your outlook or belief in things is healthy. At times, the world can sometimes feel as if it is weighing you down. Believe me, you do serve a purpose and if things are rough, maybe you need to give yourself a bit of a break to put things back into perspective for yourself. Only you know the way to do that, however.

Our health enables us to carry out our free will as mortals here on Earth. Do not take it for granted and be proactive about taking care of yourself.

~ 47 ~

FEAR

"F-e-a-r has two meanings: 'Forget everything and run' or 'Face everything and rise.' The choice is yours." -Zig Ziglar

Fear is one of our primary emotions. We learn it at a very young age. It can be an incredibly unpleasant emotion, yet it also very necessary. The feeling itself originates in an area of our brain called the "amygdala." This tiny area smaller than your "pinky" finger releases a hormone that essentially tells your body:

"Danger is present. Get out of here."

Fear comes in many forms, but the aforementioned is probably the most common. As much as we do not enjoy fear (unless you are a thrill seeker), it is essential for basic survival needs. Fear can tell you when you should get out of a dangerous situation for safety reasons, or perhaps it gives you a "jolt" of adrenaline. Either way, it is always vivid and quite a reminder that you are alive.

Fear can also be something which we choose to either motivate or debilitate us. At some point in my life, I have allowed it to do both. Zig Ziglar's aforementioned quote, in my opinion, is perfect due to the fact that how you choose to deal with fear *is* a choice.

It is not an emotion that you can run away from no matter how hard you try. It can however be extremely freeing or limiting. How can this be? Well, if you base different choices that you make in life on fear ("What if...?"), then you are permitting fear to be in control. The chances are strong that when you begin situations with "What if..." questions when considering options as form of avoidance, then you allowing yourself to give into fear. For example,

"What happens if I light this match and I burn myself?"

You probably will not light the match. Choosing to not light the match is allowing your fear of being burnt to limit the outcome of lighting the match.

Now, take the same example and begin by thinking the same thought. You get a "chill" up your spine at the thought of burning yourself, however you *do* light the match and do not burn yourself. As a matter of fact, you feel proud of yourself. Why? As much as your brain and body were resisting, you resisted against your own reluctance and overcame. Thus, you "faced down" your fear and proved to yourself that you > fear. Congratulations.

There are going to be many situations in life where fear is involved. You should think about why you are nervous about something and consider possible outcomes. Fear *does* serve a purpose. It prevents us from being too impulsive and says:

"Stop! Think before you act."

It causes one to pause and consider the situation. However, when you start to overthink is when fear can cause problems.

Bernie Parent, a former professional ice hockey player wrote a book entitled *Journey Through Risk and Fear*. Mr. Parent has a great perspective on examining and diminishing the different fears one's mind can produce. I would highly recommend his book if fear is something with which you struggle.

Just remember, fear is an emotion just like any other. It can push you forward or hold you back. It is not stronger than you unless you choose to give your fear that amount of strength. In the end, *you* are the one in control.

~ 48 ~

CYNICISM

"It is only the cynicism that is born of success that is penetrating and valid." -George Jean Nathan

I would love to tell you that cynicism does not exist in this world, but it simply is not true. The longer one lives and has different experiences, the more likely one is to become cautious. Being overly cautious and downright distrustful while assuming others' intentions are not good is being cynical.

Cynicism, generally speaking, is a negative quality. It generally causes a person's negative qualities to become much more apparent, but there are unfortunately situations in life that require cynicism.

I know people including myself who have "blindly" trusted other people. Whether it be money, favors, time, or promises, this group of people was ultimately taken advantage of in some way by another person. Senior citizens are often times victimized by con artists who scam them in some way. It is wrong, it is sad and in many cases it is avoidable. Why?

Maybe you refer to it as "having your guard up." As unpleasant as it is to admit about some people, there *are* predators that victimize other people. I am not going to attempt to psychoanalyze these types of individuals because they are not worthy of time or energy. If they choose to live their lives in that way, that is one them and I would advise them to consider karma because what "comes around, goes around" at some point, in one way or another. Therefore, if you are a good person and put positivity into the world, then you will receive good. If you are a bad person and put out bad, you are going to receive bad.

I am an optimist and while acknowledging that there are some "bad apples" out there, on the whole, I believe people are good. However, I am also a realist. Therefore, there are going to be people or situations that you cannot take at "face value." If something sounds too good to be true, chances are very strong that it *is* too good to be true.

A year or two ago, I received an unsolicited offer for a freelance job. Without going into specific details, the "job" would have taken me to Los Angeles, California for a certain company. I actually received a "paycheck" before said "job" from a different company in New York state. If I had endorsed the back of the "paycheck," I almost certainly would have become a fraud victim. I did not, however as it seemed too good to be true and I listened to my instincts.

There are numerous other instances of times I *have* been swindled or almost swindled. Now I have adopted the phrase:

"Fool me once, shame on you. Fool me twice, shame on me."

The bottom line is that in this world you have to be somewhat guarded. Not everyone you encounter in life is going to have good intentions and not everyone you encounter is going to have bad intentions either. Practice due diligence when necessary and listen to your common sense.

There is a very fine line that one "walks" between being a trusting, good-natured type person and one who becomes cynical. Beware. If you are one of the cynical ones, I am sorry if there were people or situations that made you feel the need to be cynical about everything.

The truth is that not everyone or everything is bad. I know it is not fun, especially after you have been "burned," but deep down you are probably a good person. You can still have your "guard up," but do not be afraid to let some people "in." You have to find balance to be happy and healthy in life.

THOUGHT CONTROL

"Don't let people who don't care about you, manipulate your mind, feelings and emotions or control how you think about yourself. Never give that much power to someone else."
-Karen Waddell

At the current time in which I'm living, people are literally attempting to "police" others' thoughts and speech. It falls under the idea of "political correctness." Essentially, under this school of "thought," if you think or speak something which is "unacceptable," you can become a social pariah. For example,

"If you think _____ or say _____, then you are a _____ (insert your own negative adjective(s))."

To the people that buy into this toxic way of thinking and feeling, the context in which something is said or done means nothing, a person's past history means nothing, and what they stand for means nothing. To these people, one is simply reduced to that specific negative adjective(s) based on one thought or utterance.

As sick and demented as this sounds, it is the reality of the current times and is getting worse each day. I truly hope by the time you read this, this unfortunate and dangerous "thinking" has been left in the history books.

I feel so strongly about this topic at the present time (today's date is February 5, 2020) since I know it is going to be analyzed in future history books. The United States of America is about as polarized a nation as it probably ever has been. Our government is out of control, our "news" is inaccurate and manipulated, and many citizens no longer respond to reason and diplomacy. It is simply a matter of:

"I'm right, you're wrong and are a terrible excuse for a human being for not thinking like me."

See the problem? It is toxic and demonstrates the worst sides of humanity. Unfortunately, news around the world is not much better. Even more upsetting is the passing of Kirk Douglas, one of my personal heroes, at the "ripe old age" of one hundred and three. Mr. Douglas was the embodiment of many cherished ideals: self-sacrifice, loyalty, hard work, and dedication among them. I could go on about what made Mr. Douglas and his generation "The Greatest Generation," but I will allow you to research that yourself.

Perhaps what I find so sad, disheartening and ironic is that Mr. Douglas passed away on a day that sees the country that The Greatest Generation loved and fought so hard for (The United States of America) at perhaps the most polarized and in many ways, vitriolic, it has ever been (or at least is being reported that way by the "news").

The very ideals The Greatest Generation stood and died for, namely freedom and progress, are the exact opposite at the current point in time. Sadly, it took very little time to arrive at this point, perhaps three or four generations.

Now, I am not saying at the current that we cannot get back to the point where we were, but at this undoubtedly critical junction in history and viewed through the proper lens, can be a learning experience for future generations from someone currently living through and documenting these events firsthand.

Therefore, do not ever stop questioning things or thinking for yourself. Language, in a truly free society, should not be regulated. As much as you might hate or disagree with what someone says, they still have a right to voice their thoughts. Remember, you do not have to listen to that person and they also have to endure the consequences of their speech.

However, it is very important to freely exchange ideas as it allows you to form opinions that are your own while at the same time engaging the parts of your brain related to reason and logic, two qualities essential for the survival of the human species. Remember, you might not like how someone thinks or what they say, but too many people before you came along and "paid the ultimate price" for each and every one of us to "speak our peace."

~ 50 ~

INTENTIONS VERSUS PERCEPTIONS

"Your opinion is your opinion, your perception is your perception. Do not confuse them with 'facts' or 'truths.'" -John Moore

Out of the many topics covered in this book, I believe some of the most important points belong to this topic: "intentions versus perceptions." It is, after all, how humans "read" one another and if there is an issue on one, if not both sides, there can be some very serious consequences.

When one discusses communication, there are a minimum of two people involved: the sender(s) and the receiver(s). The senders are the ones on the intention side of communication while the receivers are on the perception side.

As you may know, I work with children. Some of these children have impairments. As a result, often times when they are involved in the communication process, they either say something one way and someone else perceives it another way or vice versa. Thus, a lot of my time during the day is spent trying to explain to the children in these situations the other person's thoughts and feelings as part of their "social skills." It can be quite exhausting.

Unfortunately, many times fully grown adults who *should* know better react just as inappropriately, if not worse, than the children. If the adults are the "role models" for the children, can you see how there might be some confusion?

Every day, in my daily travels, I interact with other commuters. Even though it is usually impossible to see them due to them being in their vehicles, the communication is still there. Many people behave as if they are always entitled to the right of way and everyone else is to yield to them. Regardless of these other people's intentions, I can tell you how *I* perceive them: arrogant and selfish.

Intentions and perceptions sometimes come down to something as simple you say. You might just say "Good morning" to someone. However, your "tone" or "body language" was misinterpreted by the other person. Perhaps they were having some kind of personal issue and the timing of your greeting was not ideal for them. These things happen all of the time because we are all human. We need to be as understanding of others as we would expect them to be of us.

I would now like to like to connect the idea of "intentions versus perceptions" and how they relate to "opinions versus facts." A fact is 1+1=2. It is indisputable and the outcome is not subject to interpretation. An opinion is something which may be personally true for you, but not others. For example,

"Green is the best color."

To me personally, that is true, but maybe you do not feel that way. An opinion is not a universal truth. It is open to interpretation and thoughts can differ.

At the present time in which I live, people are conveniently passing along their own personal opinions as "facts." Some are misled into believing said "facts" while others deliberately "blur" the lines between opinions, intention, perception and reality, so they all become impossible to discern from each other. This is *not* okay and I truly hope that this current trend is discontinued.

There is nothing wrong with having an opinion about something. We all have them. However, what you need to realize is that you cannot create "alternate truths" or "relative truths." You are not any more special, unique, or entitled than anyone else. People will respect you more in the communication exchange if you begin phrases with:

"My intention is/was..."

or "My perception is/was..."

That is all any of us can do and whatever others choose to do with that information is out of our hands.

~ 51 ~

ACTIONS, NOT WORDS

"Characterize people by their actions, and you will never be fooled by their words!" -Author unknown

Many people like to say:

"I should do _____" or

"I need to _____," but then they never follow through with the necessary action(s).

Thus, actions (or inactions) speak volumes more than words ever will. Think about it: how many times have you heard yourself, or someone else state that you or they need to do something, but then never follow through? Thus, talk is cheap.

One of my earliest jobs was in sales. I remember my manager at the time, Geoff, had a motto he shared with us:

"Under promise and overdeliver." I loved the premise so much that I have since incorporated the idea into many areas of my life.

Without going into detail, one of my colleagues was recently "thrown under the bus" by another colleague. Due to one person mishandling a situation, this sweet young woman's reputation and professionalism was questioned, which is infuriating. I myself have been "thrown under the bus" many times over the years in an attempt to scapegoat me to cover their own misdeeds. Has this ever happened to you?

The one time I was betrayed to my supervisor, I took it upon myself to read her the "Riot Act." Again, without going into details about the person(s) who scapegoated me (behind my back, of course), I proceeded to tell my supervisor I was not upset at the fact that a colleague(s) had an issue with something I had done, but at the *way* it had been done. She attempted to "diffuse" my valid points with some statement similar to:

"Well, they did try to tell you (a lie) and maybe they didn't want to cause a problem."

The irony of that statement! I immediately replied that they indeed wanted to cause an "issue" in a very passive aggressive manner. I suggested to my supervisor that some perceived wrong I had supposedly committed had never been addressed with me first *before* going to the boss. To me, this was a very calculated and manipulative move on the other person(s)' part, especially as it had been done anonymously and absolutely no regard was given to how *I* would feel as a result of *their* actions.

I concluded the meeting by suggesting my supervisor have a conversation with *them* about *their own* conduct before trying to scapegoat someone else. Needless to say, in this type of situation,

"Well, I don't think that's the way they meant it" is *not* acceptable.

Everyone needs to realize both thoughts *and* actions have significant meaning. What you say and do are a reflection of *you*, no one else. When you say or do something, "own it." Accept responsibility. Even though someone else may not like something you say or do, that is their problem. Be a leader and be deliberate. Say what you mean and mean what you say.

If you make a statement:

"I am going to _____," then make sure you go ahead and _____. If you are not sure you can _____, then either say:

"I am not sure I can _____" or

"I would like to _____," but at least you are not making an "empty promise."

When I was a young boy, I told my father I was going to do something, but I did not follow through. He then told me:

"Your word is your bond."

It is a lesson I have never forgotten and ever since that day I pride myself on keeping my word. It is important for everyone.

~ 52 ~

BEING A CREATIVE PERSON

"You can use up creativity. The more you use the more you have." -Maya Angelou

Regardless of whether or not you think you are, everyone is a creative person in some capacity. Creativity does not always necessarily pertain to the arts either. It can simply be the way you approach something or in the way that you problem solve. I will say this though: If you are a creative-minded person involved in the arts, it can be incredibly difficult.

Earlier today I took an acting class with a film director who is pretty "well-connected" within the film industry. During part of the class, we began "talking shop" and how the entertainment industry is someplace where "six degrees of separation" is much more apparent than people realize.

We also discussed the personality traits of the most successful people. The traits we determined they possess are: dependability, easy-going, business-minded, and committed amongst others. The conversation then turned to life in general. It was a very encouraging, enlightening day in the fact that the group of us discussed many of ideas being discussed in this book. Why am I discussing acting?

For starters, maybe you are an actor or maybe you are not. If it is something you have never done, let me be the first to tell you it is *not* easy. I am not going to "delve" too deeply into the actual philosophy and technique of acting, but as someone who is both an actor and a writer it is very interesting to interpret the words on a page from "both sides." Sometimes, I see a script as an actor and I think,

"Well, *I* wouldn't have written this in that way. I would have written *this* instead."

However, if I am an actor in someone else's work, I only have so much "wiggle room" to give myself in my interpretation without changing their message.

It can also be very irritating at times to hear someone else say:

"You are a _____ (insert some other actor's name) type." I almost always think to myself:

"No, I am my *own* type," but I never voice the thought.

At the end of the day, it is a business and people have to know how to market their product (themselves in this case). Sales are based upon previously successful products and the individuals associated with those products. As a result, it can be incredibly difficult maintaining one's own unique qualities while being able to financially support one's self.

Just about everyone has to "sell" themselves at some point in their lives. There is a point where people want or need something from someone else and has to therefore "make a case" as to why they deserve that something. Many people are creative in the way they go about "making their case."

Anyone involved in the arts of any kind understands that there is a certain finesse and creativity necessary to have an impact. However, if your creativity is the very product you are attempting to "pitch" while using other methods of creativity to get "noticed," it can be quite exhausting.

Whenever a person releases something they created before the world, that person has to be mentally prepared that their work might not be appreciated or outright rejected. They might have spent months (or years) working on this project, only to be told it is "terrible," "too offbeat," or "not commercial enough." Anytime someone creates something that comes from a *genuine* place within side of themselves and did their best work, that person deserves to be commended.

It is *not* easy to "open yourself up" and be vulnerable to the world's criticisms. We as a people should encourage and promote *true* creativity and individuality while celebrating one another's contributions. As I have already stated, we each have something unique to offer and I cannot help but wonder what we could achieve if everyone was given the supportive "platform" required for each and every one of us to shine?

~ 53 ~

NERVES

"Nerves provide me with energy...it's when I don't have them, when I feel at ease, that's when I get worried." -Mike Nichols

Anytime I am in a situation I care about, I often times find myself feeling nervous. Guess what? That is okay! It means that I am human and that I care. If I did not care, it would mean I was indifferent, or, even worse: arrogant.

If you sit down and think about it, nerves are a perfectly natural reaction to some situations in life. We all do hopefully have a functional nervous system. Depending upon one's external environment, the brain sends signals via the nervous system faster than we could ever possibly comprehend. We truly are living, breathing miracles. Therefore, would it not be normal to sometimes feel your nerves as they do their jobs? After all, if our nerves were not functional, we would be dead since our other body systems would cease functioning.

Therefore, are we really correct when we talk about a bad case of "nerves" or "feeling nervous?" Perhaps we are being a bit too vague. Since our nervous system is so complex and vital, perhaps we should be making more specific statements like:

"Right now, my nerves are making me feel _____, most likely because of _____."

Nerves have a tendency to get a "bad rap" because we associate them with negative emotions. When your body is in a normal state or even a state of euphoria (laughter, happiness, exercise or sexual release for example), your nerves are causing you to feel sensations which are either normal or even pleasurable. However, as with anything else in life, your nervous system also informs you (or should) when you are injured, endangered, or not in control.

Are you able to "diffuse" or calm yourself down when you are in an uncomfortable situation? Maybe sing, laugh, whistle, or take a walk. I know that although I still get nervous in different situations, I have learned to calm my reactions to my nervousness and often times give the perception that I am not nervous, even though I am.

Earlier today I had an acting audition with my teacher, John. I honestly was not sure whether or not to attend the audition because I was both tired and not necessarily in the mood to travel the required distance to his studio. Additionally, I had not seen John in over a year. Nevertheless, I decided to attend the audition.

Upon entering his loft, there were at least fifteen other people present. I signed in and immediately said hello to several of my acting friends/colleagues who were also present. However, I did so quietly as we were standing in the same space where the auditions were taking place.

Unbeknownst to me, everyone was present in the same room where John himself was auditioning people. As I watched the others, it became immediately apparent to me that the original audition materials I planned on using would not be suitable. Since I am familiar with John's methods, I foresaw him throwing me some "curveballs" during my audition and I then mentally began preparing myself to remain open to the environment.

Sure enough, when my turn came, I sat in the chair opposite the "reader" (someone who sits in for the auditioning actor's eyeline) with John seated to my left and a roomful of people observing in the back. Now, let me say this: I do not care how "seasoned" someone is, but it is not natural to sit down and perform several different characterizations being given to you while several others (mostly strangers) observe. I would be lying to you if I claimed not to be nervous. I was.

However, I reminded myself that my nerves meant that I care and I used my extra nervous energy to focus my heightened awareness of my senses. I am very proud and grateful for the opportunity because any time an actor has a chance to practice with an audience, they should be grateful.

The next time you feel nervous about something, just remember your nerves can and will guide you accordingly if you "channel" that nervous energy to be your best "you" in the situation and you should be proud of your efforts.

~ 54 ~

HUMILITY

"On the highest throne in the world, we still sit only on our own bottom." -Michel de Montaigne

The best way to define humility is "to have or possess a modest opinion of one's self." Humility is the exact opposite of arrogance. Humility is a trait that everyone should aspire towards.

At the present point in time in the twenty-first century, many people have a "platform" in which to express their views on a variety of topics. Granted, there is nothing wrong with having an opinion about something provided you recognize the fact that other people are entitled to their opinion as well.

It has become quite common for individuals to be awarded with some kind of "participation trophy." Essentially, the idea of a "participation trophy" in some particular area does not equate to actual achievement in said area. Instead, to spare "feelings" everyone becomes a "winner."

The idea of "participation trophies" has come about via the practice of "political correctness," which is currently defined as "the avoidance, often considered as taken to extremes, of forms of expression or action that are perceived to exclude, marginalize, or insult groups of people who are socially disadvantaged or discriminated against."

Thus, in this type of thinking which has noble intentions, people have become "victims" of mediocrity. People are no longer encouraged to naturally excel and if they do are often disqualified because they have some perceived "unfair advantage." How does this relate to humility?

Ironically enough, "political correctness" has created an environment in which people are not necessarily the "best" in their given field are given positions of power or influence over other people. Often times, many of these same people, instead of being grateful for the opportunity they have received, instead take the time to use their given "platform" and make everything about themselves or attempt to use their influence to lecture other people about their own personal ideas and why others should act, think, or feel the way they themselves do about particular issue(s). Thus, the power of their position gives them an increased sense of moral superiority over other people, despite the fact that they themselves are *not* the "best" at whatever it is they have proclaimed to be the "best."

One thing I can tell you from firsthand experience is that being arrogant or a "blowhard" is *not* an attractive quality to possess. The second that anyone, anywhere attempts to lecture or proselytize me with unsolicited opinions on any subject I immediately "tune out" that person. First, who is this person and even more importantly, what gave them the audacity to think I even care what they have to say or think without asking me first?

Therefore, humility is an attractive trait to possess. It allows people around you to know you have a realistic opinion of yourself. You may very well be quite talented and have a lot of valuable advice to offer, but you realize that your opinion is just as valid as anyone else. You place yourself "shoulder to shoulder" with others. You probably also realize that those that brag the most usually "fall" the hardest and are later forced to "eat a slice of humble pie." Thus, in a world full of illusions, "be real."

~ 55 ~

ROUTINE

"As with most things in my life, I believe you should try to enjoy yourself and never feel like you are a slave to routine." -Donatella Versace

Most people are "creatures of habit." With routine comes structure and predictability. The interesting thing about routine is that it can be comforting, especially in new or unfamiliar situations, or incredibly boring and nerve-wracking as well.

During the work week, I have the same exact routine I follow. I take a shower after I get home from work and then get my outfit ready for the next day. Then, once I get up in the morning, I grab something to eat for my commute. I travel the same route to and from work and generally park in the same space. I go into the same lounge and eat my breakfast and drink my coffee before I am officially "on the clock." Once I am "on the clock," I typically follow a similar series of work-related tasks. Does this sound familiar to you?

As you may know, I work in a school. Some students have an impairment or "disability" of some kind. Often times, especially when discussing someone who has autism, routine is essential for them. If you have never met someone with autism, they are usually meticulous about details and often times like to plan their entire day in a particular way. Thus, it can be very difficult for someone with autism to experience some unplanned change to their schedule and can be both very upsetting and frightening for them.

Sometimes I question why there is so much structure and routine in the world. Granted, our bodies require certain routines. Yet, when it comes to areas where we have the freedom to choose what it is we would like to do, we ultimately succumb to some unwritten rule. As it is often said:

"Rules were meant to be broken (sometimes)."

The way I have come to see it, routine is necessary within moderation. Moderation is the likely answer to every area in life in which we struggle, and routine is no different.

Sometimes we have to be structured in order to accomplish something or keep ourselves within necessary boundaries. However, we can become overly rigid or structured within ourselves and thus become "too hard" on ourselves. We do not give ourselves enough "breathing room" and that is unnecessary.

Since the world is such a big place and none of us are immortal, you have to give yourself permission at times to *not* follow the rules. For example, if you eat tuna melts for dinner every

Tuesday night, is it really the "end of the world" if you eat pizza instead? No, of course not. Perhaps you are someone that likes to walk for thirty minutes every day. Well, today you did not go for a walk. Is that terrible? No. You can make up for it and walk for an hour tomorrow.

I am not a doctor, but I know that many of the ways we choose to limit ourselves in one way or another is dictated by our brains. Our brains are really fascinating organs, but they too occasionally need a bit of change to be stimulated. Guess what? A "change of pace" (or routine) is a *great* way to stimulate your brain.

Since we all know how unpredictable life can be, occasionally "changing things up a bit" can be a good exercise for your body and mind when things do not go as planned.

At the end of the day, chances are good that a percentage of the day was structured, but there also may have been a bit of variation. Think of that variation as spice, and spice is something that separates living from merely existing.

~ 56 ~

LEARNING TO LIKE YOURSELF

"Find out who you are and be that person. That's what your soul as put on this Earth to be. Find that truth, live that truth and everything else will come." -Ellen DeGeneres

I know this is going to sound strange, but I have a feeling that many people do not like themselves (or something about themselves). Pretty much every day I see at least one person do something that demonstrates either self-absorption or rudeness. The opposite is also true, but I am going to discuss the negative qualities here to highlight my point.

People say or do mean/careless things towards others. Why? I believe in the vast majority of these situations these people are unhappy with something about themselves, but they instead project their own negative feelings towards other people.

Think about this for a moment. Is it not easier to point out some flaw or failure of someone else than it is to admit about ourselves? When you point out something wrong with someone else, you have no "skin in the game" so to speak. You casually make an observation and then go about your business. However, when we honestly look within side ourselves, that can be terrifying.

It requires a lot of deep, introspective thinking and facing unpleasant realities we do not wish to admit to anyone, least of all ourselves. However, in order to grow and become the best version of ourselves possible, we have to be honest with ourselves.

No one has all good qualities or bad qualities. We are a combination of the two. Let me pause here for a second and state that if you believe you have no flaws at all, then you are a narcissist and that is your flaw. I am very aware of my flaws as I am also aware of my strengths. Truth be told, however, there are days when everyone-including me myself-really annoy me.

On these kinds of days, I excuse myself and usually go to bed. Since I am the type of person who willingly admits their own flaws, you also better believe I have no issue pointing out someone else's flaws either. It is essential to learn to embrace all sides of yourself and acknowledge their existence. Hopefully, at some point, that acknowledgement will become acceptance. Acceptance has the potential to mean you like yourself which can eventually give way to loving yourself. You should strive to like yourself at the very least.

Humans, in my experience, seem to operate in extremes. They either give themselves too much credit or not enough credit. The truth is that we are all somewhere in the middle. I realize that some people seem to be abundantly blessed and have a list of wonderful qualities that seem to never end while others can seem like a "waste of skin," for lack of a better description. What is the difference between these two groups? I believe it is the way they view themselves.

Positive people love themselves, are very "real," and usually hold a modest self-view. They know they have negative qualities, but they do not dwell on them. Their own inner light makes others around them feel good.

Negative people have a low opinion of themselves and refuse to look within. These same people often times perceive their negative qualities as attributes. They are the types of people that "suck the life out of you." No one truly wants to be around these people.

Thus, in order to be a good, functional, reasonable human being, each and every person needs to be honest with themselves about all that they are. They should try to improve the things that they do not like and let the good things about them shine through. Ultimately, in order to like or love other people, we have to be at peace within ourselves. At the end of the day, who we are speaks volumes.

~ 57 ~

BALANCE

"Balance is a feeling derived from being whole and complete; it's a sense of harmony. It is essential to maintaining quality in life and work." -Joshua Osenga

Everything in life should be done in moderation to maintain a sense of balance. There is a belief that in life for every one thing, there is something to counterbalance. Ying and yang. Black and white. Hot and cold. Up and down. You get the idea.

Our very own bodies strive to maintain an internal sense of stabilization (balance) through something called "homeostasis." Our brains definitely require chemical balances otherwise we can find ourselves in serious trouble. Yet, at times, balance can be very difficult to achieve.

You may be someone, like me, that loves to eat. The fact that I enjoy eating is not the actual problem. However, what I like to eat in excess can potentially cause many problems.

Often times, I find myself eating foods with added sugars or simple carbohydrates. Now, occasionally and within moderation, there is nothing wrong with the occasional slice of cake or bagel with cream cheese. However, when one consumes large amounts of these types of foods on a regular or semi-regular basis, the results can be catastrophic to one's health.

The same can be true of trying to stay healthy. Sometimes, people (in particular athletes who are training) push their bodies beyond reasonable boundaries. Instead of allowing themselves time to recover from intense physical training, these people's bodies begin to break down in some way.

Why do we have a difficult time finding balance in life? My personal belief is that in many, if not all cases, something in the brain is not functioning properly. Maybe there is an imbalance of serotonin and instead the normal, reasonable amount of sensory input is not sufficient enough to release these "feel good" chemicals and as a result, one over (or under) indulges.

Life, in many ways, is like a checkbook. When entering "credits," into our registers (that which makes us feel good), we also have to take into account the "debits," (that which makes us feel bad). Since we are indeed human, the laws of the universe that we study apply to us as well. Thus, this is where Newton's third scientific law would be applicable:

"For every action, there is an equal and opposite reaction."

Did you ever sit on a seesaw as a child? If so, do you remember how difficult it was to balance with someone else on the seesaw? Well, that is a pretty good analogy for life. Life has a tendency of not going at an even pace. "Happy medium" very often does not seem to exist.

Often times, life is either "all or nothing." You have to do your best to react accordingly to situations and realize that the best choice almost always lies somewhere in the middle. Extremes are dangerous, but balance almost always means peace and tranquility.

~ 58 ~

THE SIMPLE THINGS IN LIFE

"It is the sweet simple things in life which are the real ones after all." -Laura Ingalls Wilder

I realize you have probably heard that it is the simple things in life that matter, but it really is true. Life, in essence, is a series of highs and lows, often times concurrently. Thus, it can make all of the difference when something seemingly small or trivial occurs but changes the outcome of your day.

For example, today is Valentine's Day, February 14. Many of the days thus far this new year have been dreary, overcast, and rainy. Today, however, is the first day this week to be sunny and dry. It might not sound like a big deal to you, but to me this is very significant.

Although I have never been formally diagnosed by a doctor, I know I have a condition known as "seasonal effective disorder." People that have this condition are known to have their mood affected by the weather. On nice, clear, sunny days people are usually cheerful and happy. Things do not bother them as much. Conversely, on rainy, overcast days, people can be moody and depressed. Things bother them more than usual on these types of days. I know I feel as if I am two different people within the same body at times due to the different types of weather patterns.

Many people would probably view something like I just described as simple. After all, it is just a weather condition and weather conditions are not permanent. They generally change day to day or season to season. Yet somehow something as simple as the weather can affect me drastically enough that if impacts both my outlook and motivation to accomplish tasks.

In reality, life is, in a "nutshell," a "million little things" that, added together, lead to a significant amount of time in our lives. If you really sit down and think about it, most of what occurs in our happens in "steps" over time and is, for the most part, ordinary. There are extraordinary moments (birth, marriage, major life achievements) or catastrophic (death, divorce, health challenges), but the truth is that on an "average" day, there is nothing especially memorable that you are going to look back on years later and proclaim:

"Wow, that was a defining moment in my life."

Simplicity and extraordinary, by their mere natures, are mutually exclusive of one another. I am going to make an assumption and say that if you were to go ahead and ask anyone, the vast majority would agree that it is indeed the "simple things in life" which carry the most significance. Regardless of who someone is or what they do, the basic fact of the matter is that to that person, their day to day routine becomes their "normal" over the years.

Since our lives are marked by some truly exceptional events as well as heartbreaking occurrences, all of the other times would qualify as "simple times" or "ordinary times." Despite the fact that these "simple" or "ordinary" times may not be particularly exceptional, they are usually the bulk of who and what we are in this life. The "simple things" or "simple times" are really what it boils down to at the end of our time here on this Earth. The type of person you were and how you viewed these "simple times" really is all that matters when all is said and done.

~ 59 ~

RESPECT FOR ALL FORMS OF LIFE

"When people get taken over by the ego to such an extent, there is nothing else in the mind except the ego. They can no longer feel or sense their humanity-what they share with other human beings, or even with other life forms on the planet. They are so identified with concepts in their minds that other human beings become concepts as well." -Eckhart Tolle

It never ceases to amaze me just how cruel, arrogant, and downright indifferent human beings can be towards other human beings. I have never understood, nor will I ever, the level of evil exhibited by some during their time here on this planet.

I do not care who, or what, species we are discussing either. Whether it be a person, born or unborn, a dolphin, a dog, a houseplant or a caterpillar, each and every one of these beings exists and has a purpose. Whether or not others see that purpose is insignificant. No one person is the creator, and not only is it infuriating and heartbreaking when a person willfully injures or kills another living being, it is downright dangerous.

In this world, there are certain natural laws that are to be abided by. One of the most important, if not *the* most important, should be to respect *all* forms of life.

Just because you respect something does not necessarily mean you have to love, or even like it. Personally, I absolutely despise spiders but I realize they serve a purpose and if I see one, I go in the opposite direction.

When you respect something, it is a simple acknowledgement of the fact that it exists and whether you happen to like it or whether it is "personally convenient" for you, it still has a right to exist. Much of the respect for all life forms is dependent upon one's worldview. I do believe it is also important to pause for a moment and discuss intent.

There are sometimes situations, unfortunately, where someone accidentally injures or kills another person(s) or perhaps an animal(s). These types of situations are unforeseen and given to the fact that they are unintentional means that they are not the focus of discussion here. Accidents can (and do) happen to everyone. Some accidents are insignificant and others are catastrophic, but they are both accidents nonetheless.

We as a people all need to do our best and realize that not only, we, but every other form of life here on this planet, does in fact have a purpose and it is not our job (or responsibility) to determine whether or not that life is to live or die.

The "buck" does not "stop here" with any one of us humans. We are a species merely "passing through" here on this planet. Life existed long before we ever came along and will most likely exist long after we are gone. Therefore, may each and every one of us try to make the most of our time here in this life and do our part to make it nice for everyone and everything, both present and future.

~ 60 ~

HAPPINESS

"Most people are about as happy as they make up their minds to be." -Abraham Lincoln

Perhaps you are aware of this myth, but supposedly a smile requires you to use only seventeen muscles while a frown requires forty-three muscles. Whether or not that is actually true is irrelevant because one of the most important things in life is to be happy. There is so much that we see and experience firsthand, why not smile?

Life in many ways is quite absurd. We perform work to get paid in the form of money. Does money matter to any other species on the planet other than humans? We often act bizarrely and foolishly over a very strange physical act: sex. Humans walk around on two legs while other species walk around on four. We are truly a unique species.

There is a lot that happens in life, much of it outside of our control, that often times makes us want to throw our arms up in the air and cry (or scream). These are very natural, healthy responses to the issues that we face. However, out of all of the emotions that we experience as humans, why do we not spend more time on the one that brings with it true and utter joy: happiness?

As the sixteenth president of the United States noted, happiness is a choice. Sure, life at times is tough. Is life unfair? Absolutely life is unfair. Life is also in so many ways absurd, and for that reason alone we should just laugh.

It has been scientifically proven that laughing is good for one's blood pressure. It reduces stress and tension. It has also been found that forcing a smile on one's face triggers a response in the brain that you are supposed to be feeling happy. Essentially you are forcing a behavioral response out of yourself that may be contradictory to how you actually feel.

I want you to think for a moment. The people that you generally enjoy being around: are they happy or unhappy people?

Happy people generally tend to be upbeat and look for the best in a given situation. Many times, there is a common misconception that these people have not experienced hardships or challenges. I will be the first person to tell you that some of the happiest people I have ever met have also had some of the biggest challenges and most heartache of anyone I have ever met. Yet, instead of dwelling on the negative, they instead choose to focus on the positive. Therefore, happiness is indeed a choice.

Why anyone anywhere would willingly choose to be unhappy is a mystery to me. I truly do not understand their mentality. Am I suggesting that life is a "bouquet of roses?" Of course not. However, why would anyone want to internalize negativity?

Our time here on this planet is fast. Relatively small percentages of the overall population are lucky to live to at least one hundred. Now, compare our lifespan with that of a tree. One ring inside the trunk of a tree might be equivalent to fifty years, and often times trees have many of these rings. Fifty years is a long time, at least to a human.

When we sit back and reflect on the past, do our brains usually go to the negative times first or the happy ones? I honestly believe that we all need to be happy. Being happy though is a task. You have to want to be happy and if for some reason you are not, you have to figure out what it is you need to make yourself happy.

Since we do not last forever, you might as well go out and be with the people or do the things that bring you the most joy. Life is hard, but it is definitely not impossible. Therefore, every day, try to complain a little less and laugh a little more.

~ 61 ~

ALL ADVICE IS NOT GOOD ADVICE

"Never base your life decisions on advice from people who don't have to deal with the results." -Author unknown

Look around. Everywhere you turn, someone is looking to offer some kind of advice.

"Do this. Don't do that."

"If I were you, I would _____."

Sometimes the advice is welcomed. Other times it is unsolicited. Many people apparently consider themselves "experts" on a variety of topics. Always remember this: when it does not affect that person directly, it is always easy to give advice to another person. Anytime a person does not have "skin in the game," they personally do not have to worry about the outcomes.

In many cases, when people do offer advice, I believe their intentions to be genuine. They most likely are trying to be helpful, but this is important to take into consideration:

"The road to hell is paved with good intentions."

Despite what one's intentions may be, often times the outcome is the exact opposite.

A little while ago, my financial advisor, Gerry, contacted me with advice on some of my investments. Now, I have a history with Gerry, and I trust her advice on what investments are going to yield the maximum results. However, what if I was not sure about Gerry? Suppose she gave me a bad piece of financial advice? What would happen? I could potentially lose money. Even though Gerry's intentions may be what she thinks is best for me, maybe it is not the best. Or perhaps there is some unforeseen outcome?

Regardless, Gerry would not be directly affected as she would still receive her fee from me. I would be the one left dealing with the consequences. Now, Gerry is a great person and complete professional with a lot of expertise in financial planning.

Suppose however, I did not have Gerry as a financial advisor and instead had someone else. In this imagined scenario, the person does not have my best interests at heart and intentionally offers me "advice" that not only loses me money, but enriches that person. Who is to blame? Ultimately, I am to blame, although it would be easy to discuss the lack of morals exhibited by some "professionals" to deprive others of their hard-earned money.

No one forced me to take this imaginary person's advice in the aforementioned scenario. Maybe I did not "do my homework" and conduct enough research into this person or company's history before entrusting them with my money. Have you ever found yourself in a situation where you regretted taking someone else's advice? I think everyone has at some point in their lives.

Advice is something I do not take lightly. I generally try not to offer advice unless asked or ask for advice, unless I really trust the person and believe they are taking my best interests to heart. If you do not know whether or not to take advice from someone, create a hypothetical situation (do not let them know it is fake) and ask for their advice in that situation.

If the person gives you a quick, thoughtless answer, I would advise not ever taking important advice from that person. However, if they are obviously giving it some careful thought and come up with an answer similar to:

"I'm not really sure what I would do in that situation," you at least know the person is truthful.

Advice is something which is both important and personal. It is something which you should not "take lightly" and realize that regardless of the advice, *you* are the one that has to deal with the consequences.

~ 62 ~

TIMELESSNESS

"The timeless in you is aware of life's timelessness. And knows that yesterday is but tomorrow's memory and tomorrow is today's dream." -Khalil Gibran

I believe the themes of this book are timeless. I never realized, however, just how difficult it would be to write something timeless while simultaneously making it as accessible to as wide an audience as is possible.

Times change, popular culture ("fads") change, and even the language changes. I cannot possibly foresee how the world will be in the years to come, but I am making a concentrated effort to make limit my references to current popular "norms."

Often times, I will listen to, watch, or read a story with great themes throughout the story. However, unless one actually lives during the time a particular story is set, current trends of popular references have a tendency to date the story and as a result, it can serve as somewhat of a distraction.

Why does timelessness matter? Well, for the purposes of this book, I believe it to be very important. Even though the current year (2020) may seem or be a particular way, I do not want that to distract you from the fact the same issues now will also have an impact in the future.

Perhaps the current year you are reading this book is 2600. I will be long gone and perhaps the world as I know it will be unrecognizable. Nevertheless, humans in many ways I believe will be similar, if not the same as now. Thus, it would not be helpful for you to have a guide from the past to assist you with many dated references to distract you from the main ideas.

Granted, as I write this now, I cannot help but think how different the language in which I am writing, English, has changed over the past five hundred and eighty years. Although many of the ideas and messages are the same, language and communication itself continues to evolve/devolve, depending upon one's perspective. Thus, I can only hope the messages I am scribing continue to carry the same meaning and that each successive generation passes along these messages.

I cannot begin to tell you how strange it is to track the periods of human history to the present moment. One can only predict what the future may hold. For example, for generations now, people have been discussing life beyond here on planet Earth. The idea is that humans will eventually live elsewhere besides Earth.

Now, maybe by the time you read this, humans will be living somewhere else besides Earth or maybe they will not. Who knows? At the particular point in time I sit writing this section, the future regarding this specific idea is unforeseen.

However, as I stated, history is indeed a guide and I believe history teaches us that there is in fact a timelessness that connects generations. Each individual generation has its' own particular idiosyncrasies, but in the end, those very same idiosyncrasies are actually irrelevant.

Therefore, no matter when you happen to be reading this, just remember there is a "common thread" that we all possess and share and that no matter when we live, we are in fact interconnected through this common timelessness.

~ 63 ~

LIMITATIONS

"Once we accept our limits, we go beyond them." -Albert Einstein

The world often times likes to give us the message that:

"There are no limitations."

There are. No person can either have it all or do it all. I know that may not be something that one necessarily wants to hear, but sometimes we have to hear things we might not like.

Albert Einstein was onto an idea however. Even though we are limited, there is always the possibility of achieving what may not seem possible. Humans are a resilient bunch and very determined, when we want to be. Although we act within specific parameters, there is always someone who comes along and "pushes boundaries." Why do you suppose the idea of a "record breaker" ever came to be?

To debunk any theory that we are, in fact, unlimited, then allow me to pose this question: why would there be a need to "break records?" Additionally, not having any limitations would suggest that one is somehow otherworldly, and there is no human that is that spectacular. As difficult as it may be to admit, there is no one who is without limitations.

At the present point in time, the culture attempts to promote the idea that individuals can "do it all." For someone who may have self-esteem issues or happens to be very aware of their own limitations, can you imagine what an unhealthy, unrealistic, and downright irresponsible standard is being established?

The simple fact of the matter is that many people project the illusion they are *Superman* or *Supergirl*. Again, however I cannot stress this enough: these are illusions and absolutely are not realities.

Some people figure out their particular strength(s) and excel while simultaneously minimizing their weakness(es). Other people realize their limitation(s) and work on improving said limitation(s).

There is an actor named James Earl Jones. Mr. Jones was apparently someone who had a severe stutter when he was very young. However, over time and much practice, he not only achieved fame and acclaim as an actor, but he is most arguably famous for his booming, authoritative voice.

123

Perhaps the most important thing to bear in mind when discussing limitations is how to view them psychologically. If you sit around and compare yourself with someone else similar to:

"_____ is so great at _____ and I stink," then you are setting yourself up for failure. Never ever compare yourself to someone else. It is dangerous and counterproductive.

However, if you think to yourself:

"I'm really good at _____, but I'm not that good at _____," or perhaps

"I'm really not that good at _____, but I would like to get better," your self-esteem should be higher.

Regardless of what you have been led to believe, there is nothing wrong with acknowledging your limitations, as everyone should. Limitations are not something you should dwell on or feel ashamed about, but simply acknowledge their existence and move on with your life. At the end of the day, who would want to be perfect at everything? Our strengths and weaknesses are what make us unique, and what you choose to do with them is what sets you apart from others.

~ 64 ~

GUILT

"Repentant tears wash out the stain of guilt." -Saint Augustine

Since no one anywhere is perfect, it should be obvious that everyone makes mistakes. Some people are quick to accept responsibility when they make an error while others try to give the impression that they are faultless.

Depending upon to whom (and what) someone does to act in a regretful manner, the guilty party may (or may not) feel guilt. Guilt is our own internal "moral compass" which guides us to whether a choice is good or bad.

For example, you may fart in a roomful of people with a dog. No one, including you, owns up to the offensive odor and everyone blames the poor dog. Do you feel guilty? Do you admit that it was you that "passed gas?" Or do you let everyone in the room admonish the poor dog who was minding its' own business?

We live in a world which *loves* to try and make people feel guilty or inferior: for someone's income level, which politician someone votes for, a person's skin color, who someone loves, and a person who thinks or feels a certain way among many other examples. The question I have is: Who are these "morality police" and why does anyone, anywhere, give them the authority to dictate to another person what is "right" and what is "wrong?"

In case you have not already guessed, this is an area I feel very strongly about. In the current time as of this writing, I see too many people passing moral judgements on other people while their own "skeletons are falling out of the closet."

There is an old expression that people who live in glass houses should not throw stones. When other people attempt to "police" you and guilt you about something, they are ignoring their own (usually very significant) faults. It is a lot easier to "scapegoat" or "project" one's own personal issues onto another person, is it not? Yet it is also incredibly counterproductive.

My good friend Diane would say something about people that project onto other people along the lines of either: "lacking self-awareness" or they are not being "mindful." Diane is absolutely correct.

Anything that you think or feel is incredibly personal and is not for anyone else to judge. People are often their own worst critics and already experience internal conflict without others' unsolicited judgements. It is only natural for a person to become defensive and make comments towards someone else if that person first made comments about them.

Naturally, this way of thinking and acting would cease to exist if everyone took responsibility for his/her own actions. Whether or not you think someone else feels guilty or remorseful about something is irrelevant. Trying to "guilt" someone is most likely going to have the opposite effect and more often than not, that person will "tune you out."

Therefore, you worry about you and let everyone else worry about themselves. We all have free will and our own thoughts and opinions. Live and let live.

~ 65 ~

KNOWLEDGE IS POWER

"Knowledge is power only if man knows what facts not to bother with." -Robert Staughton Lynd

I love the opening quote of this section due to the fact that its' author touches on the two main ideas I would like to discuss:

"Knowledge is power" and

"Ignorance is bliss."

At the present time in world history, information is readily available with the touch of a fingertip. Anyone from anywhere in the world can connect to someone at the opposite end of the Earth. It is an incredible phenomenon, but it can also be incredibly dangerous if improperly used.

People know more about a variety of topics than any other generation in human history. However, the topics which people are knowledgeable about range from incredibly important (financial matters, global politics) to amusing ("Fifteen facts you never knew about lemurs") to downright repulsive, reprehensible or illegal (how to kill someone, "consensual" relationships between adults and children).

The access to so much information begs the question: how much information is too much information? I know a lot of people would argue that having access they want to consume is an "individual choice" or a "personal freedom." Again, I would largely agree-to an extent.

I immediately "draw the line" when having access to information that could in any way harm another person. I realize full well that there are some that would immediately argue with me about "censorship" or one's "intent." It is a very fine line and usually people do not care about how easily accessible information could harm someone, unless it is them personally.

Knowledge and firsthand experience are crucial. At the current time, many young people (twenty-five years old and younger) know about many topics. They consider themselves "experts" and often reject advice from people older than themselves. They can tell you all of the facts about some topic because they read about it, but they have absolutely no firsthand experience ("application") because they have a filtered perspective. Since they often times have "facts" and "information" passed along to them, they often do not have the necessary critical thinking skills necessary to form their own opinions about the world around them.

Another important point to mention would be the difference between being "smart" and being "educated." There is very big misconception that "smart" and "educated" are one in the same. They are *not.* Being "smart" is one's natural intelligence. It cannot be learned.

Being "educated" is learning about or being taught some topic(s) in some fashion. Some of the smartest, most insightful people who ever walked the face of the planet never went or never completed school. Conversely, some of the stupidest individuals the world has ever known had "advanced degrees," which given the level of ignorance of the people to which they were awarded literally devalues the paper said degrees were printed upon.

I will be the first to tell you that often times the "school of hard knocks" will be your best teacher in life. You learn from the world around you via interaction and through firsthand experience. There are many wonderful teachers and topics in the world waiting to be discovered and they are not always necessarily located within a school, college, or university.

There is a lot of relevant information in the world which you need to know and may perhaps even challenge your worldview. Your brain is a muscle and needs to be stretched like any other part of your body. There is also a lot of insipid or disturbing facts you may encounter that you wish you had not. The difference between being intelligent and ignorant is deciding for yourself what information is important and how it can help you to learn, grow, and expand your worldview.

~ 66 ~

BEING SELF-CRITICAL

"Self critical? Stop and ask yourself, 'Would I say this to a child or a friend?' If not, don't say it to yourself." -Author unknown

I am probably one of the "poster children" for being self-critical. For quite a few years of my life, I often held myself back from things that I really wanted to try. I played through the possible scenarios in my head and would inevitably critique something I imagined myself doing. If I actually did follow through and do something, I would decide by my own standards that is was not "good enough." However, the summer after I graduated high school, I made a promise to myself.

I remember sitting down and reminiscing over the first eighteen years of my life. I felt proud, but I also remember having regrets. The regrets I had mainly had to do with activities I had prevented myself from participating in, mostly due to my own insecurities.

The promise I made to myself on that hot, summer night of reflection was that for the remainder of my life, I was going to be true to myself and live life on my own terms. Essentially, at that moment, I said "screw you" to my own insecurities. Now, let me pause here and say those same insecurities have never gone away.

I still to this day question myself or often times find myself in some way being self-critical. The only difference between the person I am now and the person I was at eighteen is that I am now a lot more comfortable in my own skin. I realize that nothing I ever do is going to be perfect. I know I have high standards, but deep down it means that I truly care.

When any of us has any sort of doubt, it means we possess reason. We are a thoughtful, rational human being and are very aware of our own flaws. There does, however, have to be a healthy way to keep ourselves "in check."

Have you ever completed a "self-evaluation/self-reflection" form? On these forms, there are often two areas for one to reflect upon. These areas of reflection are usually titled something similar to "areas of strength" and "areas of improvement." I love this concept, because to me, it allows you to be very "real" with yourself about your strengths and limitations.

Thus, I am no longer critical in the sense that I hold myself back from doing something. Instead, if I find myself self-critiquing, it is from a mindset of self-improvement or constructive criticism. Whereas when I was much younger, I would have thought something like:

"You can't do that. You'll fail."

Now, I instead think along the lines of: "You didn't do your best. What could you do differently to improve?"

In many ways, being self-critical stems from a fear of failure. Many people are terrified of failure and thus never even make an attempt, thus severely limiting themselves in the process. I find the thought of not trying to be terrifying. I would much rather fail one thousand times at something but have the satisfaction of knowing that I at least tried.

There is going to be a point in your life where you are going to look back and reflect upon the past. You will either look back and see a person who took chances, did the things they wanted to do, and had life experience, or you will someone who "played it safe," did not really step outside their "comfort zone," from listening to their doubts, and therefore had limited life experiences. Which type of life would you choose for yourself?

SELF-DESTRUCTIVE BEHAVIORS

"Prometheus gave us fire and we use it to light cigarettes." -Marty Rubin

At some point in life, many people learn and practice some type of behavior which could be described as "self-destructive." It could be a way of thinking, feeling, or acting. For example, someone that thinks "everyone is out to get me" is self-destructive. A person who feels guilty about themself all of the time is self-destructive. Someone who eats food all of the time in engaging in self-destructive behaviors. The very real and unfortunate truth is that any type of self-destructive behavior can, at the very least, lead to unhappiness and at the very worst lead to death.

The best definition of "behavior" is perhaps:

"The way an animal or a person reacts (responds) to a stimulus."

Thus, behaviors are learned and therefore can be unlearned. There is an old expression that a person "is their own worst enemy." I believe that statement to be true. When one considers intentions and perceptions, it could be determined that these two concepts are probably the biggest cause of conflict between humans, whether it be intrapersonal or interpersonal.

People often times have a way of viewing the world around them in negative terms. Whether or not they project that negativity onto other people, themselves, or both, is dangerous and counterproductive.

Granted, many people do (or would) benefit from some type of intervention from a mental health professional(s). Often times, however, having a good doctor(s) is not in and of itself the way for one's mental health to improve. Since each and every person possesses free will, if a doctor tells a person that in order to improve, they need to do x, y, and z and the person makes no proactive attempt to do x, y, and z, then chances are good the individual's situation will not improve.

In some cases, people who are being treated in some way do not practice new behaviors long enough before deciding their treatment is "not working" and that person then discontinues their treatment.

There are also some people who may be mentally or physically (or both) incapable of taking care of themselves and who exhibit warning signs of self-destructive behaviors. In these particular cases, sound judgement calls and interventions are often required in the individual's best interests. These kinds of cases can be particularly challenging and it is very important that everyone involved do their best to promote said person's dignity and worthiness during their course of treatment(s).

Since we can unlearn behaviors, why do we not do this more often with unhealthy behaviors? Studies indicate that the brain is more "elastic" than it is often given credit for. Even for those of us with the worst, most self-destructive behaviors, there is hope and faith, even if you feel there may be none.

Granted, each and every one of us has some kind of "personal demons." Whether or not it is we ourselves or someone else that "trigger" these behaviors, please know this: you *are* loved and you *do* deserve better for yourself. Even though things may *feel* "out of control," there is nothing you cannot achieve *if* you want it badly enough. You are *not* "beyond redemption" and your life is *not* "a waste."

As I have previously stated, I realize that the world can feel like a nasty, cold place sometimes. However, the exact opposite can also be said. It can be a wonderful, accepting place with wonderful people if you look in the right places. We only get this one life and there is only one you-there will never be another. Please, if you need help, seek it and, like a horse, if someone tries to help you by leading you to water, at least try the water.

~ 68 ~

EARTH

"What is the use of a house if you haven't got a tolerable planet to put it on?" -Henry David Thoreau

I am going to be completely forthcoming with you: I am a conservationist through and through. We only have this one planet: Earth. Billions of our species alone lead our lives here.

Now, I am not arrogant enough to believe that humans can do irreparable damage to the planet. I personally believe that we as a species overexaggerate the amount of power we actually possess. However, I do believe that the effects of what we choose to do to our natural environment will continue until the end of our species as well as many other species.

Earth is truly an incredible planet. It is the only planet (of which we are aware) in our particular universe which possesses all of the elements necessary for the survival of our species. The Earth existed for years before humans and most likely will continue to exist after we are gone. Why in the world would *anyone*, anywhere want to "trash" the place we call home is beyond me.

Granted, human beings, and do, cause a lot of damage to our environment. We may have "mastered" many ways of making life "easier" for humans, but at what cost?

You may be sitting there thinking to yourself:

"Here it comes. Another lecture on what I can and cannot do."

Guess what? You are right. If you were the sole being living on the planet, I would tell you:

"Go nuts. Do whatever you want to do. It's not going to affect anyone or anything else."

The fact of the matter though is that it is *not* just you. There are many other beings either currently or in the future who will have to occupy the same living space too.

Therefore, when people complain and say there are too many lots and not enough trees, they are right. There are not enough trees. Maybe you hear there are too many pollutants in the air and water. Yes, there are. Facts are facts and the reality is that we unnecessarily pollute life for just about every species on the planet, both present and future.

I am also going to take "environmentalists" to task here, because they are a part of the problem as well. The "controlled burns" that are protested because they "destroy the environment?" Guess what? They actually prevent much worse, catastrophic fires and promote nutrient growth in the soil so new, fresh plants can grow. Many of the environmentalists' "solutions" have had the exact opposite effects intended. Thus, regardless of "intent," in many instances "environmentalists" have caused much more harm to our natural environment along with good, old-fashioned greed.

Let me ask this question: Do "good intentions" or money make a difference if there is no more livable environment? I realize it is a cynical question with extreme hyperbole, but it highlights the point I am trying to make. You are a part of the world around you and vice versa. We all have to coexist in this one unique environment. The very least we can do is to leave it in the same, if not better, condition for future generations.

~ 69 ~

SENSE OF HUMOR

"My father is a butcher, my mother cuts the meat, and I am the little hot dog, that runs around the street." -Kay Weber

Being able to laugh and have a sense of humor is probably one of the single most important things in life. I remember seeing a quote by the comedian Milton Berle:

"Laughter is an instant vacation." You know what? He was right.

I laugh and joke as hard and as often as is possible. Laughter is a wonderful distraction for your mind, regardless of the situation. It is great for calming you down and helps with one's blood pressure. To be perfectly honest, much of life in general is absurd so why not laugh? My father always says: "Life is much too important to be taken seriously." Most people also appreciate someone with a someone with a sense of humor.

It is really a gift to be able to laugh or find humor in any situation, including being able to laugh at yourself. Many times, during the course of a typical work day, I find myself laughing uncontrollably at one situation or another. Even if no one else is laughing, at least one person is happy.

Ironically enough, I often times find myself laughing harder at jokes and situations than the adolescent children I work beside. Sometimes it almost feels as if I actually find more humor as an adult than I did in adolescence.

At the current point in time, a group of elitists are attempting to control humor. Under the guise of "political correctness," the "thought and language police" believe they actually have the authority to dictate to other people what is appropriate to laugh at (and when). Of course, the very fact that these people hold these beliefs and think that anyone, anywhere, should even care about these "rules" is in and of itself hilarious.

Humor is something which is very personalized to each person and much of the humor in life arises naturally from observations or experience. For example, look at a baboon with its' reddish pink behind hanging down and try not to laugh. If you do not find that amusing, look at a picture of a "nosy monkey." I personally find both images equally hilarious and make no apologies whatsoever.

Let me be the first to tell you this: Maybe you personally do not find something funny, but it is not your job or right to dictate to anyone else what is "acceptable" humor. The more that people attempt to preach about a topic, the more likely people are to "tune them out," and laugh at that person.

The truth is that humor is an essential coping mechanism to deal with some of the crap that life throws your way. Thus, when life "throws a grenade at you," you can sit back, curl up and cry or, you can "pull the pin and throw it back" while laughing like hell. For someone like me, it is hard to imagine anything but the second option.

Therefore, try to avoid talking out of your ass as much as possible because eventually people will forget which end to reply to.

~ 70 ~

HUMAN SUFFERING

"Although the world is full of suffering, it is also full of the overcoming of it." -Helen Keller

Today is Ash Wednesday, a Christian Holy Day of prayer and fasting. It is the first day of the Lenten season, in preparation of the crucifixion and resurrection of Jesus Christ for humankinds' sins. As a way of demonstrating sacrifice and solidarity to both God and people who are poor or in some way suffering, many Christian beliefs dictate that they are to make tithes to the poor, limit their amount of food, and sacrifice at least one luxury. To put it simply, Christians are supposed to be expanding their empathy during Lent to exhibit solidarity with those around the world who are suffering themselves.

No one, however, under normal circumstances really enjoys suffering (unless they are a masochist, which is an entirely different topic of discussion). Suffering is not enjoyable, fun, or pleasant. I remember a few months back having a conversation with my priest.

I stated to my priest that I personally take issue with people throughout the world that do not want or deserve to suffer, yet they do suffer nonetheless. Father (my priest) responded to me along the lines of:

"No one wants to suffer. We do everything we can to avoid suffering but yet it is part of our journey. Suffering often times teaches us lessons which lead us to clarity and truth."

Father's words at that time made perfect sense to me. Even though we do not intentionally want to suffer, suffering is a part of the human condition. It forces a person to sit down and confront reality. Maybe it is not a part of our destiny to not suffer regarding _____ (you choose the area of life which is applicable). The suffering, in fact, is a type of lesson. We are forced to confront unpleasant fact(s) to get to the real truth of a given situation. Suffering also deepens our own humanity and understanding while allowing us to empathize with our fellow humans on a much deeper, meaningful level. Additionally, it teaches us how truly resilient each one of us truly is and highlights our natural endurance.

Thus, suffering is a part of life just as much as the more pleasant parts of reality. It is very strange to think about, but if you look at some of the situations where you have (or are currently encountering) encountered suffering, was there some kind of lesson in the midst of the chaos?

Suffering is viewed as a negative experience. The human brain has a natural way of self-preserving during traumatic events. Ironically enough though, the brain also has a way of sometimes taking the negative aspects of a situation and exacerbating them. However, if you view some negative time, experience or situation without "tunnel vision," there is probably some aspect that may have been positive. Maybe you or someone else acted in some positive, unexpected way or perhaps it gave you some kind of insight you did not previously possess.

It is natural for humans to try and escape from times when they suffer the most. While I am not suggesting to go out and seek bad experiences, I am also suggesting not trying to "run and hide" from them either. Whether you like it or not, the event(s) is happening and if you take the situation "head on and deal with it" to the best of your ability, your natural strength will reveal itself.

~ 71 ~

VOCATION

"Everyone has his own specific vocation or mission in life; everyone must carry out a concrete assignment that demands fulfillment. Therein he cannot be replaced, nor can his life be repeated, thus, everyone's task is unique as his specific opportunity to, implement it." -Viktor E. Frankl

Vocation, to a large extent, is how a person finds meaning in their life. A vocation can be one's profession, but it does not necessarily need to be. Granted, some people's professions and their passions coincide. For example, a person who truly wants to help people and make a difference in someone's life might become a social worker, doctor, nurse, or teacher. Many people might be employed in a profession that pays their bills, but which they are not passionate about.

Often times, vocation can be a lifetime search to be true to one's self or their "true calling." "Niche" would be another name for this occurrence. It can be difficult to find your way in the world, particularly if you become easily distracted or listen to *others'* dreams or goals for you.

Let me give you an example. Earlier tonight at dinner, I was having a conversation with my parents. My father told us a story about a man who was in his high school graduation class. Around the time of graduation, this man was offered full scholarships to several of the most "prestigious" Ivy league institutions in the world. What became of this man? He ended up becoming a house painter. I believe that is wonderful.

Often times, people have a tendency to please other people so much that they often times surrender their true calling in life. Society often puts immense pressure on individuals to "achieve" and thus convince a person to take an alternate path instead of that person's intended path.

For instance, suppose everyone in the world entered into some highly regarded profession. Now, for argument's sake, some arguably frowned upon profession (such as waste management) no longer existed because it was not a "favored" or "meaningful" job. Humans would have some rather serious issues if this were the case, would we not? Dealing with waste is probably a profession most people would not think of when discussing "dream jobs," but yet it serves a very practical and necessary function.

Thus, people need to realize that everyone in some way contributes to "the big picture." Although it might not seem "essential" in some way when compared to something else, everyone and everything in some way serves a purpose.

Another way to think about different jobs or professions is the economic concept of "supply" and "demand." If people did not demand _____, then there would not be a need to supply _____. Instead of judging someone else, perhaps ask yourself if what they are contributing is something from which you benefit?

It takes a very strong, independent and resilient person to be honest and true to themself. Vocation is often the way a person demonstrates his or her own individuality. Vocation and profession can be the same, but often times the opposite is also true. Your vocation in life may change over time or perhaps you feel as if you have more than one vocation, like me.

The most important question(s) for you to ask yourself is: Do I like who I am, do I like what I am doing, and am I reaching for my fullest potential under the current circumstances? If you answered "yes" to the aforementioned question(s), I would say you are doing great. If you said "no" to one of the aforementioned questions(s), ask yourself what you can change in order to reach your fullest potential and come closer to your intended self-realization.

~ 72 ~

WHATEVER WILL BE, WILL BE

"What is truly yours will eventually be yours and what is not, no matter how hard you try, will never be." -Author unknown

As I sit here writing this section, I am reminded of the song *Que Sera, Sera* by the beautiful, incredibly talented Doris Day. The most famous lyric of the song is:

"Que Sera, sera, whatever will be, will be."

Essentially, the song sums up life in one concise phrase. Yet we as humans often try to overcome fate itself. Ever hear of the word "futility?" Well, that is the most futile at anything that a person can attempt.

When I was at work yesterday, there was a young woman that led a presentation to the students entitled "Minding your mind." It was very was presented and much of what this young woman discussed with the students are the very same concepts being addressed in this book.

Although the presentation itself was aimed towards adolescents, she covered a variety of topics including "fitting in," trying to be "perfect," and gaining others' "approval." She used her own personal experiences with these topics, which is incredibly brave to make herself that vulnerable to a roomful of strangers, in an attempt to remove the stigma of mental illness and suicidal tendencies.

I was personally very intrigued and impressed by this young woman's definition of "perfection." She described it as:

"A shield, a type of delusion which doesn't actually exist."

She then went on to discuss not allowing others to determine your self-worth and finally described her thoughts concerning suicide:

"A permanent solution to a temporary problem in which you pass your problems onto people you love through one act."

Essentially, when a person commits suicide, that person dies once but the people that love that person die repeatedly. I do not think I could have worded these ideas any better and wanted to forward these same messages to you. They need to be shared.

I have heard life described like a change of the seasons. I do not think there is one person anywhere whose life turns out the exact way they predicted. Life does not always have a strict set of rules which are going to apply. You may say:

"Well, 2+2=4." Although that fact is always true in math, it does not necessarily extend to life.

In life, you may believe that you have "two" and "two" expecting to get "four," but then there is some unforeseen occurrence which alters the expected outcome. It happens to each and every one of us in some way or another.

Many of the people that know me personally remark that they are "proud" of me, that I am a "really busy guy," and a few have even said that I "inspire" them. I am not going to lie and pretend that it is not nice to receive that praise.

While it is nice to get a "pat on the back," especially in a world that can at times be unbearably cruel. The truth is, though, if I think back to when I was younger, I am definitely *not* where I anticipated I would be at this point in life. Guess what? That is okay.

I know I live my life in the way that I do to be true to myself. As wonderful as it is to have others' support, I would still be doing what I am doing even if I did not have that support. I think that is the most important message to impart to you.

I have stated this before and I will continue to state it: there is only one you. There will never be another of you in this world, ever. Like Dolly Parton once said:

"Find out who you are and do it on purpose."

Learn to coexist with other people, do your best, and handle whatever life may throw at you head first. You are enough and you are a necessary piece of the puzzle in this world. Que sera.

~ 73 ~

AGING

"There is a fountain of youth: it is your mind, your talents, the creativity you bring to your life and the lives of the people you love. When you learn to tap this source, you will truly have defeated age." -Sophia Loren

Many people have an unhealthy obsession with aging. Aging, of course, is correlated to timelines. For example, last night when I got home from work, I did not do any writing. That is the first time in sixty-nine days since I had begun the task of writing that I took a break. However, today I am actually glad that I did not do anything. My body and mind needed a break, so I complied.

As a result, my "creative juices" are really "flowing" today and my writing ideas does no not feel "forced" at all and in addition to writing this section, I completed a previous section.

Since time and aging are correlated, some might say they are the same, why are so many people obsessed with this topic? In certain situations, time is essential. For example, if someone has a medical emergency or there is a fire, one must act quickly to prevent death or permanent damage. How about those situations where there is not an emergency, however?

At the current point in time, it is a common occurrence for people to "go under the knife." While "cosmetic surgery" is not always performed to reverse the effects of aging, for argument's sake I am only going to concentrate on the surgeries performed for those who want to maintain a "youthful" appearance.

I realize many times, it can be difficult to face the reality that as one gets older, the human body shows natural signs of aging. Some people's appearance causes them to appear older than they are and sometimes a person does not look their age. Is this really relevant, however?

The fact of life is that many people in the world are denied the opportunity to grow "old." They die young and would probably love the idea of simply living to a "ripe, old age."

Although the effects of aging are often not great, there does come with it some positives: wisdom/insight, the ability to live longer and accomplish more, have longer relationships, and the ability to reflect and impart knowledge to those that want the wisdom.

Living to an older age also means you get to try more. Perhaps your life "did not really start until forty-five." Well, maybe to someone who is eighteen, forty-five seems "old," but if you are lucky enough to live until at least ninety in relatively good health, you still have (or had) forty-five quality years of life.

If we are perfectly honest, people most commonly associate aging with dying. Well, what is the alternative to not aging? Death. What is the eventual solution to aging? Death. Regardless of how you choose to view aging, death is inevitable, so you may has well have some fun as you grow older.

I remember my grandmother always used to say: "The young may die, but the old must die." Therefore, if you are seventy-five and always wanted to parachute but never have, what is to stop you? Maybe you are an eighty-five-year-old surfer. More power to you. Age is absolutely "nothing but a number." The second you let your age define you I think is the day you cease to stop living. Therefore, stop living based on the "rules" of aging and instead write your own "rules," perhaps with a bit of common sense and a doctor's consent first. Other than that, what are you waiting for? Get out there and "have at it."

~ 74 ~

TECHNOLOGY

"We are stuck with technology when what we really want is just stuff that works." -Douglas Adams

I have been waiting a while to write the technology section. Why? Well, on one hand I am attempting to write a book with timeless appeal while also doing my best to avoid dated references. On the other hand, technology is evolving so rapidly at the current point in time that it is impossible to foresee where technology is taking humans in the future. It progresses so quickly that once a particular technology becomes available for general consumption, it is already obsolete.

Before I began writing this section, I looked to see if the current time period has yet been named. The best I could locate was "The Contemporary Period," which of course is relative. Perhaps I am wrong, but I believe the current time (2020) is going to be noted in history as part of "The Technology Age." What is very difficult to determine, at this point, is if the technology age is going to in fact be the basis upon which future periods of time are set?

Technology, like many human creations, at its' best, has the truest form has noble intentions. If used properly, it can enhance quality of life, increase productivity, and allow connectivity between anyone, anywhere in the world, with the touch of a button. There are many other positive characteristics of technology as well, but I am going to limit these ideas to the ones I have already mentioned.

Technology too can also be the means of great evil or unintended consequences: loss of jobs, lack of intrapersonal communication skills, lack of physical movement, dissemination of morally reprehensible or illegal materials.

Thus, technology can either have great effects or disastrous ones based upon the individual using said technology.

Perhaps one of the most unintended consequences of technology is the negative traits it has caused in humans: laziness, indifference, impatience, physical issues, loss of critical thinking skills, loss of problem-solving skills, loss of quantitative reasoning, and a host of other deficits as well.

Needless to say, technology in and of itself does not cause these effects without willing human participants. There has been a development for many years of something known as "Artificial Intelligence" or "A.I." for short.

What is important to note, however, is that technology is not naturally occurring. It was something developed to assist humans but, in many cases, A.I. is eliminating the need for humans. There is not a single person who is replaceable, and no matter how "cool" or "convenient" technology may become, we need people.

It is truly a bizarre reality when humans and A.I. are existing side by side. As many before me have stated and predicted, there perhaps may come a point in time where the technology in the world has "evolved" to such a point it no longer wishes to obey human commands. What then?

In a time where technology is just about everywhere, everyone needs to understand it serves a purpose within moderation. Humans may have created the technology to make life "easier," but if people do not start "waking up" to the reality, the inevitable end of our species may be accelerated. However, it does not have to be. Thus, use your own brain and own body as often as possible.

~ 75 ~

DEATH

"Life is a moderately good play with a badly written third act." -Truman Capote

Death is a really strange topic. Humans are born, live life, and then finally "kick the bucket." We are one of the only species on Earth, if not the only species, that are aware of our own eventual mortality. Some people dwell on death and are terrified. I personally prefer Frank Sinatra's observation:

"You better get busy living, because dying's a pain in the ass."

What is it about death that captivates us so much? Most people would say it is the unknown.

When I sometimes discuss the topic of death with others, they are surprised when I mention I have no fear of death. It may sound strange, but I truly do not fear death, unlike my intense fear of spiders. Granted, I am a very spiritual person and believe in the afterlife.

Death can be annoying however if you really think about the topic. If you are the type of person like me that likes order and tidiness, you like to try and control the circumstances of different situations. Of course, the very idea that we have control over such things is absurd and as much as we might like to be in control, we ultimately are not.

Death is not something in which I think there is a "perfect" way of "transitioning" from this life. There is no perfect way of dying, inevitably there are things we would forget to say or people we forget to contact, and not every issue can be resolved. Truly, the list goes on and guess what: that is life! Death is a part of the life cycle. We live to ultimately die. Very peculiar.

What if, however, we did not die? My father introduced me a while ago to the story *She: A History of Adventure* by H. Ryder Haggard. In the story, the title character has access to a specific fire. Once one steps into this fire, they become immortal and live forever. However, if one steps into this fire a second time, they die and are immediately reduced to ash.

While the idea of immortality is intriguing, I personally think that living on Earth for too long would eventually become tiresome. Even though one could potentially experience many different lifetimes, at what point would "a lot" become "too much?" To me, the novelty would probably wear off quickly, especially given the different "seasons" of human existence here on this planet.

If you existed for say one thousand years, and both the human species and world was completely different and unrecognizable from the way you knew it when you were young, would you not feel like an outsider and miss the world as you had originally known?

Simply put, I personally believe that most people probably experience enough in their rather limited time they have here on Earth. There gets to be a point in one's life (if they have lived long enough) where they get tired and likely miss loved ones that have passed on before them.

While the concept or physical act of death in and of itself might not be appealing, it is probably for the best that it is an occurrence to which everyone eventually succumbs. Therefore, live each and every day to its' fullest and enjoy being in this middle act of your life for however long it may last.

~ 76 ~

HUMANS ARE ONE SPECIES IN ALL OF CREATION

"If you ever start taking things too seriously, just remember that we are talking monkeys on an organic spaceship flying through the universe." -Joe Rogan

Have you ever seen a graphic of a particular person on Earth where the camera keeps pulling back until the focus is at the other end of the universe? It seems to be a bit of a dichotomy that even though each being is important, we are also infinitesimally small on the "grand scheme" of things.

As of right now, on planet Earth, there are at least seven billion humans in 2020. How many other species do you suppose there are on the planet Earth?

Take this idea and expand upon it even further. There is a sun, eight planets, one "dwarf" planet, countless stars, meteorites, and many other elements in this one universe. As of the present, it cannot be accounted for whether or not there are other universes as well. How big do you feel now? My guess is that, at best, we would maybe account for the size of one grain of sand on the beach.

Are we as humans really that spectacular? Well, I guess it depends upon your perspective. If you are the type of person that likes to see yourself as the "center of the universe," then yes, perhaps you are spectacular. If you are the type that chooses to view yourself as one tiny piece of an incomprehensibly large puzzle, then maybe you do not find humans all that spectacular.

My personal belief is that we most likely fall somewhere in the middle. I think we have the potential to be spectacular in certain ways in our given spot in this particular universe, but who knows how we compare to the rest of creation? Therefore, I like to try and "take it all in stride" and like Joe Rogan suggested, it is really best not to take it all that seriously.

FAITH

"We are twice armed if we fight with faith." -Plato

I looked at several definitions of the word "faith" before writing this section. My favorite definition is:

"Belief that is not based on proof."

Human beings have been programmed to find logic everywhere. After all, we have five senses to allow us to experience the world. Even when there is no discernible logic in a given area, we try to explain the given phenomenon. "There has to be a logical explanation," someone might say:

"We just need to gather more evidence and look at the facts."

Granted, there are some events that humans will never be able to explain. For many, this is where faith begins.

An atom is the smallest unit of matter. It cannot be detected with any of the five senses nor is there an invention that can isolate an atom. Yet, through scientific methods and some mathematical equations, it has been determined that atoms are, in fact, real despite not actually being able to see them.

Often times, humans attempt to disprove beliefs, ideas or events as "invalid" due to them "not being able to be proved by science." By this logic, anything not able to be proved by science is simply a "fluke" or "invalid." Guess what? Often times, some forms of science invalidate other types of science. You see, much of human logic is derived from "proofs." The "scientific method" itself has become a proof. However, it is not exact nor precise because science is often based upon theories or elimination of other factors. Many conclusions are reached based upon the "fact" that if _____ is true, then _____ cannot be true (or vice versa). This, in many ways, is itself based upon faulty "logic," but is often presented as "fact."

Now, you are probably thinking that I personally do not like science. Nothing could be farther from the truth. I believe that science is absolutely essential in explaining different phenomena on Earth and beyond. However, I do have a problem when people claim that science and science alone explain everything.

Humans were born with free will. It is only natural that in an attempt to explain existence, there had to be some formal way of exploring and testing different ideas about existence. Science is the natural answer. However, it is an evolving field and many ideas and concepts are not concrete.

In life, there are going to be many experiences that science cannot explain. Yet, if you believe them regardless of what your logic or human intuition tell you, then you have faith. There is really no way of explaining faith other than the fact that there is an innate sense that you have about some phenomena.

Sometimes though, people who have a lot of faith attempt to discredit science. Thus, let me say this: science and faith are not mutually exclusive of one another, nor should they be. Often times, science will act as a type of "friend" when identifying the root cause of an illness and the cure. Conversely, if you ever need some kind of operation or "procedure" performed and the doctors tell you there is no scientific explanation for your positive outcome, then that is where faith intervenes. Like Plato once wisely observed:

"We are twice armed if we fight with faith (and logic)."

~ 78 ~

MORALITY

"The purpose of morality is to teach you, not to suffer and die, but to enjoy yourself and live." -Ayn Rand

At the present, "moral relativity," as it is known, is very common. As a result, both life and quality of life in many cases have been cheapened to complete insignificance. You might hear a person say:

"Don't judge me" or

"Who are you to judge?"

Let me pause for a second and say that there is a difference between judging a person and judging a person's action(s). No one should judge a person. However, providing insight about a specific act(s) is another matter.

There is an old saying to be "good for goodness sake." I absolutely agree. In the current time, some people belong to an "organized religion" and many do not. Many people associate religion with a belief in that which is holy. "Religion," however, is defined as

"An organized system of beliefs, ceremonies, and rules of a group used to worship or govern."

Thus, not only are Judaism, Hinduism, Christianity, and Islam religions, but so are secular ways of thought such as atheism and paganism. Many times, individuals who identify themselves as "atheist" or "agnostic" often associate a type of perceived (im)moral behaviors with individuals that claim to lead their lives in way which conflicts with the teachings of "their God." You know what? Many atheists and agnostics are correct. There are many hypocrites and bigots who do "cast stones" in the name of "God," but that is where spirituality needs to be separated from religion. Religion is open to human interpretation and rules whereas spirituality is very personal and unique and specific to an individual and their belief(s).

Thus, when discussing morality, the concepts of "good" and "evil" are dictated by the difference between "right" and "wrong." How does one distinguish between "right" and "wrong" or "good" and "evil?" Enter the Ten Commandments. These ten rules, as prescribed by God, are ten written rules each person is supposed to use as their guiding principles:

1.) I am the Lord thy God, thou shalt not have any strange gods be Me.

2.) Thou shalt not take the name of the Lord thy God in vain.

3.) Remember to keep holy the Sabbath day.

4.) Honor thy father and mother

5.) Thou shalt not kill

6.) Thou shalt not commit adultery

7.) Thou shalt not steal

8.) Thou shalt not bear false witness against thy neighbor

9.) Thou shalt not covet thy neighbor's wife

10.) Thou shalt not covet thy neighbor's goods

There you have them. Ten simple guiding principles to live by. Whether you like it or not, many of the laws of the land are based upon the Ten Commandments. For example, murder and theft are illegal.

As long as there are humans, there does need to be a basic template to coexist; otherwise, if there were not, chaos would ensue because there would be no rules. Rules have to be in place for members of a species to inhabit the same space, and humans are no exception. Thus, the Ten Commandments are the basis of morality for humans to abide by, and it has nothing to do with belief or religion. It has to do with necessity.

You can be a person who states that they do not believe in a higher power or that you are not sure. That is your right. It is not any other person's place to condemn you for your personal beliefs nor is it your place to condemn theirs. However, in order to have some order for humans to live, the rules of basic morality (The Ten Commandments) must be adhered to in some way for everyone to be held accountable for their actions in an equitable way.

~ 79 ~

GOD

"There is no one who is insignificant in the purpose of God." -Alastair Begg

I waited to write this section of the book last. Not because God is *ever* last, but because I wanted to have a clear focus in my writing. God is *never* last in my life. He is *always* first. As a matter of fact, the only true guidance I get in life is through God.

No matter what I do, what I think or what I say, I know God loves me unconditionally. He loves me in a way that I could never love myself. Any good I achieve in life is a direct result of God's influence.

I know that many people reject, ignore, or insult God. Many people act as though God is full of wrath (another of the Seven Deadly Sins), but that is not at all what I envision when I think of God.

Our life on Earth is very fast and a mere "blip on the radar" before hopefully spending (if you believe like I believe) an eternity in God's presence in paradise, Heaven. My perception of the afterlife was forever changed when I read *What Dreams May Come* by Richard Matheson. In order to perceive the ideas presented in this story, you have to disregard the very notion of what it means to be human and "open yourself up" to other planes of existence. I cannot personally recommend the story enough.

As a human being, it can be incredibly difficult to comprehend the very idea of God. Therefore, I am not even going to attempt to lecture you on God's existence, but simply explain to you how incredible and remarkable God the Almighty truly is.

It seems beyond comprehension, but God (or some higher power if you prefer) *is* responsible for all of creation. How or why things happen may seem relevant in this life, but I believe we leave them all behind when we "cross over" to the next life.

Sometimes our plans for ourselves in this life do not happen because they were not part of *God's* plans for us. The sooner we resolve ourselves to this idea, the easier it is to accept and surrender.

As much as there is a God, there is also an evil force, the Devil. Here is a prayer to Saint Michael the Archangel:

"Saint Michael the Archangel, defend us in battle. Be our protection against the wickedness and snares of the devil; May God rebuke him, we humbly pray; And do thou, O Prince of the

Heavenly Host, by the power of God, thrust into Hell Satan and all evil spirits who wander through the world for the ruin of souls. Amen."

God has a very unique relationship with each and every person. Just because God may feel like He is not there does not make it true. As hard as it may be, we at times are tested (sometimes more than others), and as much as we might want resolution, we are not always going to get what we want in the way that we want. However, and this is the part that probably every person struggles with at some point, God *does* love you and pain and suffering is never permanent.

I truly feel that once we pass on from this life, there is yet another one, where things *are* perfect and that besides God, everyone and everything that we ever loved is there. However, we *have* to do our best here on Earth in this life to be rewarded in paradise.

Often times, atheists will say to me that once we die, they simply think we close our eyes for the last time and there is nothing more. I would much rather go *knowing* that there *is* something, then pass away *thinking* there is not but finding out differently.

God is truly remarkable in the fact that He loves us in spite of ourselves. There really is no way of ever truly being remotely deserving of His grace, but if we "play our cards right," we get to be in His presence forever. *That* is the only *true* perfection.

~ 80 ~

FINAL THOUGHTS

March 4, 2020

"We are all passengers on the train of life. The only thing we don't know is when or where our destinations occur or where they lead. Therefore, sit back, try to relax, and enjoy the ride." -Shawn Shillingford

Well it is difficult to believe, but today is my last day of working on the rough draft of this book. To put it into perspective for you in case you have a personal goal of some kind, it took me seventy-four days to transcribe my thoughts. If you want something bad enough, you *will* find a way to make it happen.

As personal as writing the book has been, the book itself is not about me. It is not about you. It is about *all* of us. Granted, I had to use a lot of "first person" language and personal experience to personalize the book and make it relatable, but I am sure you can find yourself on many of these pages.

Needless to say, attempting to write a "self-help" guide for life is a very lofty goal. To my personal knowledge, such a broad literary project from this perspective has never been told in this particular way.

I had no specific "template" or any way of knowing how to start or where to end. I am sure there are topics I omitted or could have expanded upon, but at the very least the idea was to have this book as a reference guide.

There are *so* many resources in this world and I encourage you to seek out as many for yourself as possible. You may notice I wrote this book in a conversational tone and that the book itself is *not* perfect, nor is it intended to be. What kind of message would I be sending about the imperfections of life if the book delivering that message was flawless?

Some parts of the book I think turned out great and "flowed" so to speak, while others feel as if they "dragged on." Thus, the very topics I was writing about often reflected my current mood while writing and the attitude I personally feel towards many of the topics.

I deliberately did my best to alternate the "good" with the "bad" in this book. There might be some sections you love and some that you hate. You might "skip" to a particular section or sections, or perhaps read the book from cover to cover. It very much has to do with *you.*

I intentionally wrote this book in a straightforward manner: it is not always going to be what you *want* to hear, but what you *have* to hear, like it or not.

Regardless of how you perceived the presentation of the ideas contained within, I want you to know that this book was written from a place of love and pure intentions. However, the way this book is received is truly none of my business. I hope you view it as a "pep talk" of sorts, maybe when you need one the most.

Although much of this book references acting, you have to understand that is a topic that *I* personally am passionate about and have somewhat of a perspective on. You may or may not be an actor yourself, but acting in its' truest form reflects the human experience and all of the topics presented herein are not only relevant to acting, but to life as well.

I really hope this book inspires some kind of positive change in your life. If even *one* person is affected for the good, then this journey will have been worthwhile. I invite anyone who would like to add ideas to feel free and make this book a type of "woven tapestry." It truly exists for all of us collectively.

In closing, faith, happiness, dreams, and relationships is what, for me, everything "boils down to." Look around at everything else in life we humans have to contend with. Therefore, simply be and always remember: the best perspective is to find perfection in life's imperfections.

~ 81 ~

THE UNPLANNED

March 26, 2020

I am adding this section as a warning. In the few weeks since I have completed this book, there has been a worldwide "pandemic" or "outbreak" of a virus being referred to at the current time as the "coronavirus" or "COVID-19." Despite it being inevitable that there was going to eventually be another widespread epidemic of some kind, the onset of this public health nightmare has many unforeseen implications which may unfortunately impact the world for years to come.

Many people throughout the world are now being mandated to stay inside, "life as well know it" has been suspended for an indefinite amount of time as of this point, millions of people are either currently infected or have succumbed to this particular virus and vital supplies are scarce.

Making matters worse, many people have actually turned the situation into a sick joke by *not* complying with the necessary precautions to prevent the spread of this virus and the number of examples of people either intentionally trying to spread this highly contagious and deadly virus or trying to contract the virus literally defies logic.

People are intentionally "hoarding" needed supplies and many of the aforementioned individuals' actions are directly and unnecessarily impacting the length of time and course this outbreak is having on the worldwide society.

Many people are also being true heroes and despite their own personal fears are going on and trying to help as many people as possible. It simply is not logical for me to attempt to write everything that has occurred during this period of time, as I am sure there are going to be countless materials for years to come as well as new guidelines to prevent something with as devastating an impact as this current "coronavirus."

Why am I adding this section to the book? Well, I am not attempting to be an "alarmist," but in such a short period of time in world history, various events that too many people disregarded as "highly unlikely" to happen *have* indeed happened.

Thus, it *should not* even have to be stated, but you *need* to wash yourself *every* day, cough and sneeze into your elbows or somewhere where germs cannot be spread, and just be a normal, responsible, decent human being. If you read about this in the future *after* this period is over and you did not personally experience this situation, let me tell you this: it is a situation that *did not* have to become this severe but has due to many people's flat out indifference and arrogance towards other human beings.

I *truly* hope this trend to completely be narcissistic and put the wants of one's self ahead of the needs of society as a whole soon ends, but it may eventually become a matter of law where people are dictated as to what constitutes acceptable and unacceptable behavior.

Thus, if you or someone you know values "if it feels good, do it" above all else, refer to this current turning point in history as to why that mentality is not only selfish, but downright dangerous as well.

~ 82 ~

SPECIAL THANKS

It is impossible to compile a list of every inspiration I have ever had in life that led me to write this book, but God I know led me to write this book. God leads me to everything in my life which is good.

Furthermore, I want to thank my parents Lisa and Chuck, my grandparents, all of my family, and my friends. I guess really anyone pretty much I have ever encountered in my life, past, present or future as they have or will impact me in some way or the other. It should also go without saying that I thank you, the reader, more than you could ever possibly know.

~ 83 ~

OTHERS' QUOTES

Since I wrote this book for everyone, I also invited others to share quotes that they thought would be beneficial for you to bear in mind. They are shared below:

"Here's to the words we throw up on the page/and call art." -Megan Anderson, from her poem "More Than Grammar"

"Be true to yourself!" -Elyse Bard Goldberg

"Love always hopes!" -Karen Blankley Arcuicci

"It's not about how big the house is...it's about how happy the home is." -Chemita Cedeno Pega

"Not all broken families are miserable. And not all complete families are happy." -Chemita Cedeno Pega

"When you are full you refuse honey but when you are hungry even bitter food tastes sweet." -Chemita Cedeno Pega, as taken from Proverbs

"It is impossible to know your true potential when you give up." -Krista Cesarine

"Happiness is as the butterfly. If you can catch it in your hand, you must either let it fly away, or keep it and watch it die." -David Croft, OBE

"Idol hands are the devil's workshop." -Jackie Davis

"It's not getting what you want, it's wanting it after you get it." -Jackie Davis

"When the going gets tough, only the tough gets going!" -Chadwick Grahams Jesse

"My imperfections are what makes me imperfectly perfect! Love yourself and others will follow." -Susan Hall-Prince

"This too shall pass." -Sue Lawley Steinmetz

"Please listen to the warnings from the world, not everything you hear is a conspiracy." -Jessica Moyer

"People find new ways to hug." -Ellen Newton

"Something worse than being attacked is attacking yourself." -David Ogrodowski

"The key to unlock self-help involves a person seeing all of the dreams inside themselves and what special gifts they have to bring to the table. Everyone has something special inside them waiting to be opened like a gift and created." -Sheryllynn Santini

"Up not down, love always." -Nancy M. Schwartz

"You will only regret the things you didn't do." -Jeremiah Shaffer

"Times of uncertainty and fear bring out the best in humankind. Never forget how bad it was and always live your life with compassion, gratitude, tolerance and faith." -Lisa Sorrentino

"You have to want it more than you're afraid of it, whatever 'it' is for you. You can only be as honest with others as you are with yourself." -Madison H. Stanton, M.Ed.

Life is not easy. Perfection does not exist in life. Therefore, understand that it is okay to be human and make mistakes. The contents of *Finding Perfection in Life's Imperfections: It's All a Matter of Perspective* is a guide to life.

Shawn Shillingford is the author of *You Never Know...* and *Finding Perfection in Life's Imperfections: It's All a Matter of Perspective.* Mr. Shillingford is also an actor, filmmaker and educator.